Advance Praise for *Financial Fresh Start*

"In *Financial Fresh Start*, Shari Olefson provides her readers with the information necessary to thrive in the new American economy."

—John DiBiase, National Association of Realtors, Government Affairs Communications Director

"*Financial Fresh Start* gives us invaluable advice on how to recover from America's mortgage and debt crisis."

—Manny Munoz, Co-Host/Executive Producer, South Florida's First News AM 610 WIOD and 100.3 FM

"In an age of information overload, *Financial Fresh Start* cuts through the clutter and is essential reading for everyone seeking to put their personal finances on a strong foundation or help their small business to thrive. The recent waves of financial regulations are easily explained and put in perspective so that you don't need a degree in economics to understand them."

—Sean D. Foreman, Ph.D., Professor of Political Science, Barry University

"Shari Olefson has provided the consumer a practical how-to guide to navigating today's uncertain and highly regulated consumer financial climate."

—William Sklar, Director, Institute on Real Property Law, and adjunct professor, University of Miami School of Law; Co-Chair, Governor Bush's Homeowners Association Task Force

"*Financial Fresh Start* contains essential information every American needs to know."

—John Bock, former offensive lineman, Miami Dolphins

"It can be overwhelming trying to keep up with all the financial and consumer news that really matters. In her new book, Shari Olefson breaks down the complicated subjects, focusing in on what you really need to know. These nuggets come from a trusted expert with no agenda other than making America even better for our next generation."

—Roxanne Stein, news anchor-reporter, WPTV-TV NBC

FINANCIAL FRESH START

Your Five-Step Plan for Adapting and Prospering
in the New Economy

SHARI OLEFSON, J.D., LLM

⫶AMACOM

AMERICAN MANAGEMENT ASSOCIATION

New York • Atlanta • Brussels • Chicago • Mexico City • San Francisco
Shanghai • Tokyo • Toronto • Washington, D.C.

Bulk discounts available. For details visit:
www.amacombooks.org/go/specialsales
Or contact special sales:
Phone: 800-250-5308
E-mail: specialsls@amanet.org
View all the AMACOM titles at: www.amacombooks.org

This publication is designed to provide accurate and authoritative information in regard to the subject matter covered. It is sold with the understanding that the publisher is not engaged in rendering legal, accounting, or other professional service. If legal advice or other expert assistance is required, the services of a competent professional person should be sought.

Library of Congress Cataloging-in-Publication Data

Olefson, Shari B., 1963–
  Financial fresh start : your five-step plan for adapting and prospering in the new economy / Shari Olefson. J.D., LLM.
      pages cm
  Includes index.
  ISBN 978-0-8144-3229-7 -- ISBN 0-8144-3229-8 1. Finance, Personal. 2. Recessions. I. Title.
  HG179.O44 2013
  332.024--dc23

                          2012044632

About AMA

American Management Association (www.amanet.org) is a world leader in talent development, advancing the skills of individuals to drive business success. Our mission is to support the goals of individuals and organizations through a complete range of products and services, including classroom and virtual seminars, webcasts, webinars, podcasts, conferences, corporate and government solutions, business books, and research. AMA's approach to improving performance combines experiential learning—learning through doing—with opportunities for ongoing professional growth at every step of one's career journey.

Printing number

10 9 8 7 6 5 4 3 2 1

For Devon and Brooke,
my inspiration for all that matters most.

—xo Mom

Contents

ACKNOWLEDGMENTS

Writing a book, in some ways, feels similar to what I suspect infidelity might feel like. Particularly as deadlines approach, weekends, evenings, and virtually every spare moment in between are spent "cheating" on your spouse and kids to be with your book, essentially putting the good—the value you hope to add for readers—above your own family's needs. And so, now that *Financial Fresh Start* is complete, it seems appropriate—okay, downright necessary—to say "thank you" to my entire household, including our dog Zoe, for your patience with dirty laundry, the litany of other chores that went undone, take-out dinners instead of home-cooked meals, and for tolerating gazillions of early mornings and late nights at the computer. Naturally it takes more than even the most wonderful, amazingly supportive family in the world to bring a book to life. Enter Bob Nirkind and Chris Murray, professionals, mentors, and confidants extraordinaire. These guys epitomize passion, drive, and untiring support--on occasion reminiscent of a strict high school principal, and they completed the proverbial circle, helping to create what I believe you will find to be a truly worthwhile book. Finally, there have and continue to be many people working hard every day to help insure that America and American's just like you get their fair shot at an intelligent and successful financial fresh start. Please check out the online acknowledgments at www.askshario.com/acknowledgments so we can be sure these folks get the credit they well deserve.

INTRODUCTION

A very simple question: If you think back to ten or twenty years ago, how common was it for you to know or regularly hear about folks in foreclosure, or folks deciding—strategically—not to pay back their debts? What about cities and towns going bankrupt, or huge financial institutions and even entire countries being bailed out?

What about now?

What Does It Mean?

As the mother of two teenagers, I often wonder how commonplace these sorts of things will be ten years from now and exactly what that will mean, not only for our personal finances, but for our kids and the legacy and country we leave behind for them. Is America still the greatest nation in the world, or does it just look that way because other countries are, at least for the time being, worse off?

My own childhood includes memories of my grandfather, a New York City fireman, sitting at his desk every Saturday morning and writing out checks by hand to pay his bills. Maybe you have memories like that of your own parents or grandparents. Everybody used good old-fashioned cash, and so people were acutely aware of how much money they did or did not have. And, of course, it goes without saying that they would never dream of spending money they didn't have. Back then, alternatives beyond accepting responsibility and consequences for your own financial decisions didn't even occur to folks, and they certainly would never have expected to be given the opportunity for a full-fledged financial fresh start. In fact, I still remember the day my grandfather made the final payment on his home loan. He and Nana invited the neighbors over for a BBQ and literally burned their old tattered mortgage papers. America was built by folks, like my grandparents and perhaps yours, who believed in their own power to make their lives better.

Fast-Forward to Today

Today we talk about how complicated banking, borrowing, investing, and finance have become. Yet the truth is that some of the same simple values that kept our grandparents out of trouble still apply today and probably always will. Timeless golden rules such as "Don't sign anything without reading it first," "Be careful who you trust," and "If it sounds too good to be true it probably is" could have saved a whole lot of folks, banks, and even entire nations a whole lot of hassle these last few years. While we learned important lessons by watching our own parents or grandparents literally count their pennies, today's kids spend money on iTunes purchases with a single click. And millions of American children will sit at their dining room tables tonight, listening to their parents talk about their homes and their banks and whether they can (or want to) pay their obligations. These are the kind of intangible impressions we are instead making on our own "next generation."

In fact, if you fast-forward from my grandfather's day to today, for some folks it feels a little bit like financial Armageddon. As an attorney on the front line of the real estate bubble and the bailouts and Great Recession that followed, I can tell you that all of those detailed clauses in all of those legal documents that folks, including you, have signed over the years—you know, the ones that used to be explained away with the naïve assurance, "Don't worry about that clause; it talks about economic circumstances that will never really happen"—have indeed happened.

Thanks to the bubble, bailouts, and Great Recession, and the decades of lesser-known unsustainable economic trends that preceded those historic events, folks across all demographics are trying to regain their financial footing in an America that now has less opportunity for upward mobility than France, Germany, Sweden, Canada, Finland, Norway, Denmark, and a host of other nations. Those born into America's middle class today are statistically more likely to move down the economic ladder than up! The life-changing impact on personal wealth and sociofinancial safety nets is undeniable. And here's the kicker: Unlike our grandparents, who had very little or nothing to lose, many of us were *born* into the middle class and now actually have a lot to lose. The fact is, our middle-class clock is already ticking. Where home equity was once the cornerstone of personal wealth for two-thirds of the middle class, 2007 was the first year ever that banks owned more home equity than homeowners did. Ninety-five percent of the jobs lost have been middle income. And more than half of today's middle-class students graduating with a bachelor's degree are jobless or underemployed. Truck drivers, retail salespeople, and fast-food workers are among the biggest job opportunities predicted by the year 2020. Not that there's anything wrong with those jobs. They're all honorable positions. But they're not the first jobs that come to mind when we think about the promise of opportunity and upward mobility for a college graduate.

Everybody's financial circumstances are unique, but the common denominator is that no matter how fat or thin your own wallet, you can *always* make your personal financial position even better (and you certainly never want to make it worse!). As you dodge your own financial bullets (or, if you're fortunate enough to be financially comfortable as you watch other folks' retirement plans, investments, and dreams blow up), big corporations and the very rich are paying professionals to keep them abreast of all the new rules and reforms coming out of Washington in the wake of the bubble, bailouts, and Great Recession. But for mere mortals like you, being uninformed translates to disadvantage, missed opportunity, and the enhanced potential of moving down that socioeconomic ladder.

The Good News!

The truth is, where there's adversity there is always opportunity. (Feel free to visualize a Broadway production complete with raging war. Suddenly, the metaphoric heroine begins emerging from the rubble, angelic, with soft stage lighting, triumphant music rising in unison from the orchestra below ... now back to our own reality.) When average Americans stopped paying their mortgages they brought Wall Street to its knees. Talk about the power of the people! The challenge is harnessing that same power for your own and America's betterment. The silver lining today, as you will very quickly see in Chapter 1, is that the Great Recession brought those decades of unsustainable economic trends to light. And best of all, it has given everybody a once-in-a-lifetime opportunity for a fresh start. It is precisely this financial mess that is driving, first, an unprecedented second chance to correct any missteps you may have made and get your own finances back on track and, second, opportunities to get even further ahead, the likes of which you may never see again.

If you want to pull yourself out of the line of financial fire, take advantage of these opportunities, and get yourself on the best financial path moving forward—voilà, here's *Financial Fresh Start*! They're doing it on Wall Street and in banks, financial institutions, and corporate boardrooms. They're doing it in Washington and governments across the country. They're doing it in Europe and around the world. And in five simple steps you can do it, too!

What ... Exactly ... Is New?

So what exactly is new? For starters, we now have more than 2,000 pages and 400 brand-spanking-new rules and reforms being written under the Dodd-Frank Act and, more recently, billions of dollars in settlements, including the "robo-signer" case (in which banks and servicers, among other things, allegedly falsified signatures, titles, and documents). In between, we have hundreds of new laws, regulations, pending legislation, programs, initiatives, lawsuits, investigations, and even new authorities such as the Consumer Financial Protection Bureau, most of which impact your money and all of which are explicitly crafted to give government, private enterprise, and folks like you a fresh start. Your banking and borrowing; your credit and debt; your savings, investments, and retirement; your homeownership; your spending and earning; even your education, training, and employment—the new economy, rules, and reforms touch it all. To protect yourself and prosper, no matter who you are and your exact situation, you need to know the new rules of the game. You need not only accurate but actionable information. But you're already busy, so you need it fast and easy!

Enter the Five Simple Steps!

Financial Fresh Start simplifies intimidating subjects—financial, legal, real estate, cultural, historical, political, and economical challenges and changes—showing you exactly how to get your "mojo" back in five simple, strategic steps, and with a style that engages, empowers, and inspires … and with none of the hidden "agenda" you may find from professionals (whose real motive is to get your business), politicians (who, of course, want your vote), or the media (who, at the end of the day, are all about ratings). In a single holistic resource, you get exactly what you need to know (nothing more and nothing less) to adapt to new rules, reforms, and historical changes and prosper in America's new economy. You'll learn what these new rules, reforms, and changes mean, why they matter, what to expect, and how to keep your head above water today and get yourself and your family ahead during the coming years.

Your fresh start begins with a brief 50,000-foot aerial view of the big picture, what happened in America and what it's doing to your money, followed by a quick summary of the new changes, rules, and reforms and what they mean to your wallet. Then it's off and running, applying this knowledge to your five simple steps.

Step 1: Adapt Your Banking and Borrowing

Do the new rules and reforms in banking and borrowing really make these aspects of your financial life less costly and more transparent, or is the whole thing just a game of musical chairs? There's little doubt that, for many folks, the new rules and reforms mean less access to low-cost loans and credit. In essence, everybody is paying more so that those at the subprime end of the banking and borrowing spectrum can be treated more equally. Your home loan, student loan, car loan, small business loan, even your credit cards are all impacted by the new rules and reforms. Now, more than ever, reading the fine print, particularly in mail from your credit card providers, is a must if you want to protect yourself from higher fees. At the end of the day, taking ownership of your own banking and borrowing behaviors is unavoidable, and step 1 prepares you to do just that, so you can take advantage right away, applying what you've learned to **your banking and borrowing**, including your car loan, student loan, small-business loans, even your credit cards.

Step 2: Fix Your Credit and Debt

It may not be easy, but improving your credit and debt is time well spent. It allows you to move forward with your fresh start plan without the risk of either credit or debt becoming an insurmountable obstacle to your future prosperity. And you will find that once you've achieved getting your debt down and your credit score up, you are far more motivated to keep it that way! Step 2 shows you how to get your financial life back into balance, cleaning up **your credit and debt** under the new rules and reforms.

Step 3: Protect Your Savings, Investments, and Retirement

The adage that nothing is certain in this world of course holds true for your savings, investments, and retirement, and even more so under the new economy, rules, and reforms. But at least some financial planning is better than none at all. For most folks, that means keeping it simple: diversifying among and within the five basic investment categories; maximizing your retirement vehicles; and keeping a watchful eye out for telltale signs in interest rates, inflation, tax legislation, and the new laws governing your money manager. Step 3 guides you through all of these fresh start opportunities under the new economy, rules, and reforms, ensuring continued protection of **your savings, investments, and timely and comfortable retirement**.

Step 4: Decide If Homeownership Is Right for You

It wasn't long ago that the homeownership vs. renting debate was a no-brainer. But in the new economy that's not the case for everybody anymore. Some folks are questioning whether homeownership is right for them or even a solid place to invest their hard-earned money. The new shorter-term "triage" rules and reforms are intended to help keep people in their homes. But it's undeniable that the new longer-term rules and reforms, and certainly the new economy dynamics surrounding homeownership in general, risk changing the role that homeownership has historically played for Americans—perhaps forever. These changes alone may have far-reaching implications for America's middle class (who rely more heavily on home equity for their personal wealth), but also for everybody else who, as stakeholders (and taxpayers) in America, may very well wind up paying the price for the shortfall if the important role of home equity is allowed to fall by the wayside. Roughly 90 percent of Americans self-identify as being middle class, so this is no small price tag! If you decide to include homeownership in your financial fresh start, step 4 shows how striving to own your home free and clear is the way to go. And why keeping an eye out for new rules and reforms from Washington that impact homeownership is a wise way to make sure your most valuable investment remains safe. Step 4 helps you navigate the challenges and new opportunities in *your homeownership*. If owning is not for you, then even if you are renting you can learn how to protect yourself and even leverage real estate investing opportunities under the new economy, rules, and reforms.

Step 5: Earn More, Spend Less

Americans have more expenses that we consider to be "essential" in the new economy than ever before, particularly as a result of technology and everybody's need to stay electronically connected in so many different ways. Step 5 delivers proven strategies for cutting your "biggie" spending and ensuring that tools you think save you money (like loyalty and reward programs) actually do. And you'll learn about the many opportunities in the new economy to earn more moola. America was built on individualism and hard work, the exact same qualities that will seal the deal on your personal financial prosperity and make your country great again. Step 5 gives you surefire ways to **spend less and earn more** as you move forward under the new economy, rules, and reforms, guaranteeing a balanced budget with money left over to sock away for your prosperous tomorrow!

But that's not all. *Financial Fresh Start* provides you with invaluable special features: tips and tools you can count on to help you find the right professional help, safely avoid the scammers, and lock in the best return on your investment in education, training, and employment. If that's not enough, you'll find even more in the online Appendix at www.askshario.com/financialfreshstartappendix, so be sure to keep this URL handy! If you want quickly accessible solutions to the challenges keeping you awake at night, you want a financial fresh start.

This is not my grandfather's America. He never heard of Christopher Dodd or Barney Frank. And he would have never dreamed that foreclosure could be anything but a humiliating disaster. The rules of the personal wealth and finance game have changed. Americans have different, never before imagined expectations and challenges in the new economy. In some ways that's good and in some ways it's bad. *Financial Fresh Start* simplifies all of it so you can decide for yourself how you want to take back the power of your own finances and ensure that the legacy and the country you leave for your children and grandchildren is one that you can be proud of!

PART ONE

Where We Stand

CHAPTER ONE

Getting a Handle on Your Big Picture

- **What Will You Learn from This Chapter?** This chapter connects the dots for you by explaining what the heck happened in America and around the world in financial markets and how the meltdown has impacted your own financial situation. You'll also be introduced to the new rules and reforms created in the wake of America's Great Recession. You'll learn what they are, what they really mean, why they matter, and what you can expect next.

- **How Will This Knowledge Help You?** Being uninformed translates to disadvantage, missed opportunity, and a higher likelihood of facing more financial obstacles. After reading this chapter, you will have the basic "need to know" background and broad-stroke understanding of the new rules and reforms that impact every facet of your fresh start plan toward financial prosperity.

First, a Look Back

A fresh start is all about moving forward. But the path you decide to take and, more important, where that path will take you depend on where you are starting from and what is going on all around you as you journey forward. This chapter sets the stage for your own personal fresh start by explaining what the heck's been happening around you, undetected, right before your eyes—economically, politically, culturally—that has ultimately climaxed in the financial challenges confronting you today.

In many ways, these worries are the very things you are feeling (but perhaps can't quite put your finger on) that keep you awake at night. What's been happening to your income, expenses, assets, and debts? What about the country's finances? What does what happens in other parts of the world have to do with your finances? How do the reforms and new rules from Washington in reaction to the Great Recession impact you? How can these rules and reforms help you rebuild your prosperity? This knowledge will allow you to understand the big-picture backdrop behind your current financial situation (and the nation's) and also understand the broad strokes of the rules and reforms that emerged from America's financial challenges.

And this chapter will more easily identify elements you need to incorporate into your own fresh start action plan, so you'll be better able to adapt to inevitable changes to rules and reforms and prosper in the new economy.

Why America's Economic Evolution Matters to You

If you're like some folks today, you find yourself "checking out" when discussions turn to the economy. Partially because—let's be honest—

it sounds a tad boring, or maybe things just seem to have gotten too complicated. But it's also because it feels as if there's not much you can do about the economy anyway. The general assumption today is that rich people, big companies, and politicians control the economy. Average folks like you have no say in these things, right?

Wrong! Knowing the basics about what's going on, the buzzwords you should be listening for, and what you can safely ignore are all imperative to making the right choices in your own plans for achieving your own financial goals. In fact, perhaps most ironically (as you will soon see more clearly), it is oftentimes the everyday American whose behavior actually determines the course of the economy. Take, for example, the way banks and Wall Street panicked in 2008 and America's government and politicians woke up and sprang into gear when average Americans on "Main Street," just like you, stopped paying their home mortgage loans.

America's economy matters to you because, in many ways, the country is like a *company* and you are one of "The America Company's" shareholders. When The America Company is in good financial shape, the benefits of its success flow to you as a shareholder in countless ways. For example, you may wind up paying less for your own healthcare because The America Company can afford to provide you with some of those services. Or maybe you get a break by not having to pay income taxes on the money you spend on childcare, again because The America Company can afford to run its business without needing that extra cash from you. The financial health of The America Company sets the pace for pretty much the entire business climate, which translates to *your own* financial situation. When the country is doing well, there are direct and indirect and immediate and long-term ways you wind up with more money in your own pocket and a better shot at improving your own financial situation.

But the opposite also holds true. When The America Company faces financial struggles, you get less from it, and the country's struggles, one way or another, wind up costing you hard-earned cash in more ways than you may know.

The connections between America's economy, your own financial situation, and some of the ways you can protect yourself and your money will become clearer for you very shortly. For now, suffice it to say that even if conversations about the economy feel alien, overly complicated, redundant, or boring, there is no denying that America's economy has a very direct and very big impact on your personal financial situation and your own life, plans, and goals. Fortunately, the few things you really do need to know about America's economic evolution in order to protect yourself and prosper are simple. And you can rest assured that this discussion will focus only on basic, "must know" aspects of America's economy that are easily accessible and immediately useful to you and your personal financial situation, and we'll do that together in under ten pages.

America's Financial Goals Are Just Like Yours

If you're like most folks, your top financial priority is ensuring that your income exceeds your expenses so that you can pay your bills and make ends meet. In the bigger, longer-term picture, your goal is ensuring that the amount by which your income exceeds your expenses continues to grow so that you can enjoy an increasingly robust lifestyle, build up your savings and investments, and pay down any debt you might have accrued, so eventually you won't have to worry about money and can retire on time, all without feeling like you're sacrificing. Is that really too much to ask for? The term *upward mobility* is commonly used to describe this shared vision. And, over time, it has become an expectation that Americans often simply assume will come to fruition.

This same big-picture goal holds true from one generation to the next. You no doubt want your children's financial situation to be even better than your own, just as your parents and grandparents wanted the same for you. After all, isn't that the essence of the American Dream?

The same broad-stroke financial goals apply to America's economy. Like most Americans, notwithstanding the fact that your own financial situation takes precedence, you presumably want your country's economy to continually improve over time. No one doubts that America will face occasional temporary setbacks, but in that big picture, over the long term, your preference would presumably be that America's economy continually improves, if for no other reason than the fact that when The America Company's financial situation is good, you know that more of *your own* cash stays in *your own* pocket and achieving *your own* personal financial goals tends to be a smoother sail.

Like most folks, you gauge your own financial situation by how much you earn (your income), the bills you pay (your expenses), how much you have in savings or investments (your assets), and how much you owe to lenders or creditors (your debt or liabilities). You can easily gauge America's financial condition the same way. Terms like *gross domestic product* (GDP) and *standard of living* help describe these measures of America's economy (see sidebar). Standard of living tends to go up or down when a country's gross domestic product goes up or down. When GDP goes up, America's businesses tend to earn more and expand, which means more jobs and more folks being able to spend more money. This translates into more taxes being paid to The America Company (taxes are *income* to America, see Figure 1-1) and further growth and opportunity for you to earn more income as well. In fact, this all translates to your own financial situation, including your own job security, savings, and investments. Stock prices, for example, tend to go up over time as the GDP goes up. If, like most folks, your retirement savings or pension fund is invested in the stock market, positive GPD puts more money in your pocket! So while productivity, which measures how much a country produces by the manpower it took to produce it, and GDP do not measure America's income per se, they do provide an indication of how healthy America's income—including taxes from companies, workers, and folks like you—will be.

Conversely, when GDP numbers go down, that's a red flag for you to listen up and pull out some of the strategies you'll learn in this book to protect yourself. As you will see, even drops in GDP can create opportunities if you pay attention and you know where to look.

Figure 1-1. The America Company's income comes in the form of taxes, most of which is from folks like you.

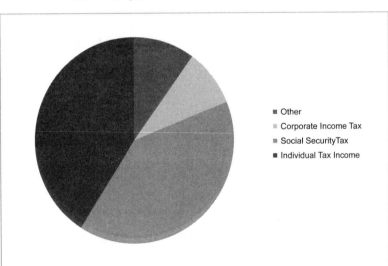

One-Minute Mentor: GDP and the Standard of Living

Gross domestic product (GDP) is the total of everything produced in the country—in other words, all goods and services. GDP is sometimes expressed as the difference between the current gross domestic product and the gross domestic product the last time it was measured. For example, if gross domestic product is down one and a half percent since last year, it is expressed as -1.5 percent.

Standard of living means all of the wealth, material goods, and necessities available to you (and other citizens in the country) that make for a quality life. Income, housing, healthcare, education, political and religious freedom, your chances of getting a disease, and environmental quality, among other factors, are all used to measure standard of living.

What Went Wrong?

So here's the puzzling question for you: If, as you will see shortly, America's gross domestic product has continually gone up, then what happened that caused your own financial situation, the financial situation of millions like you, and America's entire economy to take a turn for the worse with the Great Recession?

Like all aspects of economics, there are endless theories, opinions, and debates on the topic of what caused the challenges you're facing in the new economy. My book *Foreclosure Nation: Mortgaging the American Dream* explores this subject in detail. While discussing all of them exceeds the scope of this book, quickly recovering those you can control is relevant and will benefit you tremendously in the coming years.

No doubt, you know about the "housing bubble" and so many of the money troubles that began when that bubble burst. But some experts believe many of your own (and the country's) money troubles may have actually begun long before the housing bubble ever inflated.

The Income Piece of the Puzzle

After the Great Depression of the 1930s and all the way up until the 1970s, America's workers were rewarded for growing GDP and productivity with increased income in the form of wages. True to the country's shared vision of upward mobility, hard work paid off for the country's workers. And since two-thirds of America's economy depends on average folks spending their money, a behavior referred to as *consumer spending,* a large portion of these wages wound up being recirculated into the economy, to the benefit of all Americans and the country itself.

During the last three decades of the twentieth century, GDP and productivity continued an upward climb. But something different began happening to the wages of America's workers. Instead of increasing at a healthy pace along with productivity and gross domestic product, as had long been the case, wages paid to America's workers increased very little. There are a multitude of theories for why this shift occurred. What's important for you to know is simply that it happened and that in the years since, contrary to income increasing over time, as would be needed in order to achieve the upward mobility everyone wants, America's workers have instead actually been earning effectively *less and less* over the past few decades.

The Expense Piece of the Puzzle

Your financial situation includes both income and *expenses*—what you make and what you spend. I just explained what's been happening on the income side: Average Americans actually earn less today than a decade ago. The other part of this particular puzzle involves how much money Americans have been spending. Many measures are available to illustrate the expense piece of this puzzle, including:

- *Consumer Price Index (CPI),* which measures movement in the price of goods and services purchased by a typical consumer like you.

- *Inflation,* which is a rise in the price of the goods and services that you buy. With inflation, your money buys fewer things than before. The groceries that previously cost you $100 a week, for example, now cost you $150 a week. Of course, if you're not earning more money, that can be a problem. Phrased conversely, inflation erodes the buying power of your money.

- *Deflation,* which is a decrease in the price of goods and services. With deflation, the value of your money—in other words, what your money can buy—increases. Deflation sounds like a great thing, right? But it can actually be worse for the economy than inflation. Think about what happened in America's housing market beginning in 2006. Home prices "deflated" by as much as 50 percent in some areas. Homebuyers were afraid to buy because they thought that home prices might continue dropping, and as a result, many sellers could not sell their homes. In other words, deflation may reduce the value of things you want to buy, but it can also decrease the value of all things you already own to below the amount you invested. When that happens to everybody at once, the result is not pretty.

For more information on these terms, see the video clip at www.askshario.com/terms.

The bottom line is that since the 1970s, the income of average American workers has not kept pace with their expenses. As a result, more and more Americans found it difficult to make ends meet. But as it turns out, they were sitting on a treasure chest from which they could continually borrow money to cover this silent shortfall: their homes. Unfortunately, the "solution" quickly became the problem.

Turning Assets into Debt

During the decades leading up to the housing bubble, around 65 percent of Americans were homeowners, and all this happened while the value of American homes continued to grow, eventually accounting for the majority of the average American homeowner's personal wealth. As such, home equity has long been the leading financial safety net and nest egg for Americans. Economic pressures, however, began to take their toll. Whether it was the need for extra cash to make ends meet or desperation to accumulate enough money to retire, Americans began to rely on borrowing, siphoning off their precious home equity to pay for things that used to be paid for with their wages—and draining their personal financial safety nets and nest eggs in the process.

If you're one of the folks who began to rely on borrowing, you know how addictive it can be. Once you start, your spending habits adjust to having that additional money and it becomes increasingly difficult to cut back your spending again. Borrowing of this magnitude occurred in millions of homes across America. And, knowing this, banks of all shapes and sizes leveraged the opportunity to increase their own company profits by keeping the lending spigots flowing. Folks took on car loans, student loans, and credit cards; they borrowed in a variety of other ways until, eventually, the average American household was spending 120 percent of its income. All the while, The America Company's debt was also on the rise.

You know what happened next: With mortgage loan money readily available, home prices escalated through the roof, creating a housing bubble that eventually burst at a cumulative loss in home value and personal wealth to Americans of more than $13 trillion.

Why the Mess Spread

The housing bubble provides a great example of how the impact of an economic bubble bursting can quickly take on a life of its own, spreading deep and wide into other areas of the economy. What first began as a default and foreclosure problem for folks with *subprime home mortgage loans* (riskier loans generally made to less qualified borrowers and lower-end or speculative homes), eventually spread to *all* home mortgage loans, borrowers, and homes. America's government tried to intervene, but nothing seemed to work. Eventually everyone's home values began dropping and an economic cycle referred to as *adverse feedback* began.

Adverse feedback is a cycle that, in the case of America's housing, began with home mortgage loan defaults and foreclosures. Those foreclosed homes eventually sold for lower prices, dragging down the value of surrounding homes. As surrounding home values dropped, the owners of many of those surrounding homes, likewise, began defaulting on their own home mortgage loans, causing further foreclosures and home price drops, and so on and so forth. Over time, this cycle gained momentum, becoming increasingly difficult to stop.

As home values plunged, folks realized that all they had left was the debt. In other words, not only did Americans lose the *wealth* (assets) they thought they had accumulated in their homes, but they also became saddled with unprecedented *debt* (liability), with no way in sight to pay it back. While some people realized what that situation would mean to their personal financial situations right away, for others it has taken months, even years, to fully understand.

Eventually, the effects of the housing bubble then spread into other areas of America's economy, sucking in folks like you who may or may not have even engaged in risky home purchases or borrowing.

One familiar example of this horizontal spread is the rise in America's unemployment, creating a second adverse feedback loop. As home values dropped and folks felt poorer and stopped spending money, company sales naturally dropped. Companies, even those not impacted directly but simply "spooked," in turn cut back on production and on costs, including the cost of employees. Many folks ended up unemployed or underemployed. Those folks (and others concerned about the bad news and the potential for more of the same) in turn cut back even more on spending money (some even defaulting on their home mortgage loans), further fueling the adverse feedback loops in both housing *and* unemployment.

Because real estate and construction accounts for as much as 20 percent of America's economy and employment, when the housing bubble burst, the effect on employment was especially rapid and acute. Not only did America's unemployment rate grow, but the length of time many folks have remained under- or unemployed has also skyrocketed.

The Global Economy

As America's housing bubble grew and then deflated, other countries around the world began seeing similar phenomena. Like America's own housing bubble, there are a wide variety of reasons that housing bubbles and recessions occurred in these other countries around the same time.

What's important for purposes of the financial fresh start is noting the timing. The fact that these things happened around the world at approximately the same time illustrates how inextricably interconnected the economies of countries around the world have become, hence the term *global economy*. That means that some of the things that happen in Greece, Portugal, or Spain may very well impact America's economy and your own financial situation and, therefore, are best not completely ignored. The reverse is also true: What happens in America affects the world. The housing bubble was one of those globe-changing events.

America's Debt Takes a Pounding

Remember that financial prosperity, for individuals and nations, depends on expenses not exceeding income. Unfortunately, the housing bubble exacerbated an already-growing problem with The America Company's expenses—and, subsequently, its growing debt.

First, the housing bubble increased America's expenses (which had already been high due in large part to military spending on wars and Homeland Security) with trillions of dollars in commitments, guarantees, investments, and expenditures (including the infamous "bailouts," which I'll address shortly). There was hardship on the *income* side of America's financial puzzle, too, as companies and workers earned less and thus paid less in taxes. America's long-growing trade deficit has also added to the country's financial troubles on the expense side (a country that imports more than it exports is essentially buying more than it's selling).

Finally, there is the serious structural problem of entitlements, such as Social Security and Medicare. The price tag for entitlements has quickly risen. Social Security is the biggest expense in America's budget! The problem is that the money to pay for it comes in from working Americans' payroll taxes, and the expenses—the Social Security "benefits"—are paid out to Americans who no longer work. As baby boomers retire and more of them collect Social Security and live longer, but fewer folks are working to fund the Social Security program, shortfalls or deficits are bound to occur.

What's important here is that this ongoing mismatch between expenses and income has contributed to America's growing debt. For a long time, America's approach to its debt problems has been to simply borrow more, rather than forcing the American government to live within its means, as everyday folks like you must do. America borrows by issuing *United States Treasury securities,* which can be compared to IOUs. The money investors pay for these securities is used to run the country. In return for investors lending America money by buying these securities, America pays its investors interest and pays back the principal when it comes due.

America has a stated maximum amount that it can borrow. This is the now infamous *debt ceiling.* The ceiling, however, is not really a ceiling since America's leaders can—and must (if they don't want to default on the debt)—raise it to cover America's expenses.

Just as you strive to keep your credit score high, United States Treasury securities have always had a stellar credit rating. But in 2011, when the country came so close to defaulting on repaying its debt (by not raising the debt ceiling), the credit rating agencies were not happy and lowered the credit rating of U.S. Treasury securities. How does this event affect you? A lower credit rating generally means higher interest rates for everyone, which means it costs *you* more to borrow.

Responding to the Crisis: Demystifying the New Rules and Reforms

You can see how, over the past few decades, America's financial stage has been set for a dramatic climax (and perhaps why you yourself are now facing certain financial challenges). That dramatic climax, according to some folks, was the bursting of the real estate bubble and the Great Recession that followed. Now that the economy has captured everyone's attention, taking full advantage of the chance to get a fresh start and set things right seems like a smart next step. (Clearly, that's what you're doing for your own personal financial situation, as is evidenced by the fact that you're reading this book.) But what is America's government doing with this valuable fresh start opportunity, and as America's leaders develop new rules, reforms, and initiatives in Washington, D.C., what will their choices mean for you in the coming years?

The answers to these questions can be found within those new rules and reforms coming out of Washington. As is the case with so many things in life, you will see that there are two sides to every new rule and reform. On the one side, there are deliberate outcomes that the new changes are designed to achieve. On the other side are all of those other impacts the new changes ultimately also wind up accidentally causing. Sometimes these accidental impacts, called *unintended consequences,* do not become apparent until after the new rules or reforms have had time to sink in. Therefore, anticipating and preparing yourself for unintended consequences can sometimes be even more important than preparing for a new rule or reform itself.

The bad news is that there are a seemingly never-ending number of new rules and reforms. The good news is that there is no reason on earth that you need to know every single thing about every single one of them. In fact, the smartest way for you to approach demystifying the new rules and reforms is to, instead, focus on the reasons behind them and the broad-stroke *themes* that are most likely to affect your own personal fresh start. You'll have the opportunity to quickly drill down as much as you need into those specific areas that are most relevant to your own personal situation when, in the chapters that follow, you are guided smoothly through a process for crafting your own fresh start.

Are The America Company's Problems Really from the Big, Bad Bailout?

It should come as no surprise to you that the main reasons for the new rules and reforms (and the themes they follow) can be traced to the bailout. If you turned on the television, picked up a newspaper, or tuned in to a radio station at any time during October 2008, you heard all about the bailout of Wall Street and America's financial institutions that were considered too big to let fail. The Emergency Economic Stabilization Act of 2008, enacted on October 3, 2008, commonly referred to as the *bailout* of the U.S. financial system, was a law passed by Congress that allowed the government to spend up to $850 billion to rescue America's financial institutions (which, for reasons of simplicity, I'll sometimes collectively referred to as "banks").

Among the causes that put these financial institutions at risk were heavy investments in home mortgage loans (as discussed previously in this chapter), which American homeowners could no longer afford to pay and which, therefore, began going into default and foreclosure. These mortgages had been *securitized* through a process that, in its simplest form, involves putting a lot of mortgages together into a pool and then selling investors the right to receive a piece of the cash flow (the collective incoming mortgage payments each month) from that mortgage pool. Because these securities are based on payments from mortgages, they are called *mortgage-backed securities*. To complicate matters further, many of the buyers and sellers of these mortgage-

One-Minute Mentor: What Are Derivatives?

In most basic terms, a derivative is a contract between two parties where one party agrees to pay the other upon the occurrence of certain events (for example, if the mortgage loans behind mortgage-backed securities go into default). A *swap* is a special kind of derivative in which one party (for example, an institution that has invested in mortgage-backed securities and is concerned about the risk of borrowers defaulting) exchanges incoming payments from its investments for another institution's investments. In a *credit default* swap (CDS), the second institution essentially agrees to step in and pay the mortgage loans if, for example, the mortgage loan borrowers default.

backed securities were also participating in even more complex deals called *derivatives* with other institutions and investors (see sidebar).

If the financial institutions that had indirectly invested in America's home mortgages in the manner just described were allowed to fail, many believed that the financial contagion would spread to other institutions around the country and around the world. It may be helpful for you to picture this interconnectivity as a big ficus tree with invisible roots and visible branches stretching endlessly, far beyond the mere tree trunk. When America's leaders decided to bail out the financial institutions that had engaged in mortgage-backed securities, derivatives, credit default swaps, and other "risky" behavior, it was not because their actual tree trunks were too big to fail, but rather because of the fear that their visible branches and invisible roots had spread financial contagion to endless other institutions and investors that, together, rendered them too big to allow to fail.

The $850 billion bailout is important when explaining the broad-stroke themes behind the new rules and reforms, because never before has so much of your public taxpayer money been spent for private business purposes—and America does not want that to happen again.

Thus, notwithstanding the fact that decreasing wages of America's workers and America's growing debt contributed so significantly to the Great Recession that followed—facts that are acknowledged time and again in today's political discourse—the lion's share of new rules and reforms instead focus far more on reining in and punishing potentially risky business and bad guys at banks and other institutions than they do on increasing worker wages and reducing The America Company's debt. You may naturally wonder how much of the new rules and reforms are influenced by politics as usual—in other words, what politicians perceive as the issues that will win favor and get them reelected and good old-fashioned turf wars among regulators—as opposed to actually making the best possible use of The America Company's fresh start opportunity in ways that will benefit average folks like you. After reading this chapter, you will be better equipped to decide that matter for yourself! In the meantime, the following overview will give you an idea of what new rules, reforms, and initiatives will be available so that you can quickly choose the ones you may want to include in your financial fresh start. And the best news is all of this will be quickly summarized for you in under ten pages. So hang in there; you're almost ready to jump into your own personal five-step fresh-start plan.

Two "Buckets" of New Rules and Reforms

Focusing on the broad-stroke themes, virtually every single one of the new rules and reforms falls into one of two simple "buckets":

"Triage" Rules and Reforms. The first bucket contains shorter-term rules and reforms aimed at stopping the financial bleeding, so to speak. More particularly, the goals are to immediately keep folks in their homes; keep buyers buying new homes; and keep banks lending, businesses and employment growing, and mortgage money (and other types of credit and loans) flowing.

"Long-Term Care" Rules and Reforms. The second bucket contains longer-term rules and reforms aimed at more permanently fixing the bigger systemic fault lines that supposedly necessitated the bailout and caused foreclosures and other problems; these reforms are also focused on punishing the bad guys.

Short-Term Triage Rules and Reforms

The new shorter-term rules and reforms perhaps most relevant to average Americans now concern housing and are broadly focused on three basic objectives:

1. *Preventing Foreclosures.* The objective is keeping folks in their homes with foreclosure alternatives, including home mortgage loan modifications, or helping them exit gracefully with short sales, for example.

2. *Stabilizing Communities.* Lower- and middle-income neighborhoods, in particular, tend to be harder hit when the economy tanks, and, in this case, many of these neighborhoods will never fully recover.

3. *Using the Clout of Fannie Mae, Freddie Mac, or FHA.* The objective here is to accomplish a variety of shorter-term triage, such as temporarily lowering the credit score you need in order to get a Federal Housing Administration (FHA) loan, so that home mortgage loan money remains available to more borrowers and homes continue to be bought and sold.

Preventing Foreclosures

The vast majority of foreclosures following the housing bubble can be attributed to 1) troubles that folks are having paying a high monthly home mortgage loan and 2) unemployment. For this reason, most of the new short-term triage initiatives designed to prevent foreclosure dealt with housing-related financial problems and employment-related financial problems.

Although there are plenty of new rules and reforms that relate to homebuying, by far the most widely known shorter-term housing triage is the Making Home Affordable initiative. President Barack Obama described Making Home Affordable (MHA) as the "centerpiece" of the administration's housing recovery strategy, initially claiming that it would help 9 million Americans. You may have heard of the Home Affordable Modification Program (HAMP), for example, one of several programs under the Making Home Affordable program. It has been tweaked time and time again in attempts to improve its effectiveness, but, some will say, these adjustments have sometimes caused more confusion than good. The various programs of the MHA initiative will be covered in more detail in Chapter 5.

There are also new government rules and reforms under these fresh start opportunities if your challenge is job-related. Perhaps the most well-known program if you are unemployed or underemployed (which simply means that you are making less money than you were before) is the Hardest Hit Fund—$7.6 billion administered in eighteen states and the District of Columbia through each state's Housing Finance Authority. If you need help paying your mortgage while you are unemployed or underemployed, or even if you need help getting caught up on your home mortgage loan once you get a new job, this and other new rules, reforms, and initiatives are out there waiting for you. The individual states set their own criteria for disbursing the Hardest Hit Funds they are given, but there is a fair amount of similarity from state to state. Rest assured, if you or someone you know is struggling with unemployment, the next chapters will give you tools to access this triage resource, too.

Stabilizing Communities

For better or for worse, the adverse impacts of the housing bubble, foreclosures, and the Great Recession have not been evenly distributed across all demographics. Folks in lower- and middle-income brackets have been harder hit and in bigger numbers.

For this reason, after "preventing foreclosures," the second shorter-term housing triage focus is new rules and reforms aimed at "community stabilization"—and it tends to be directed toward neighborhoods dominated by lower- and middle-income folks. Among the most well-known community stabilization triage initiatives is the Neighborhood Stabilization Program, which is disbursed in four rounds totaling billions of dollars. This money is used to provide counseling, affordable housing, and related services.

Using the Clout of Fannie Mae, Freddie Mac, and the FHA

The final core housing triage focus for new rules and reforms is on Fannie Mae, Freddie Mac, and the FHA. These government-related entities are important because of the leverage they have over banks and servicers (the companies that banks hire, sometimes actually owned by or affiliated with the banks, to manage your mortgage loan on a daily basis). Both Fannie and Freddie are part-government, part–private sector, shareholder-owned entities the government can control. They're often together referred to as the GSEs, which stands for "government-sponsored enterprises." Fannie and Freddie insure, buy, and sell pools of mortgage loans that banks have made to folks like you. They either keep the loans in their own investment portfolio or resell them to investors in the form of mortgage-backed securities. Banks like the idea of pooling and selling mortgage-backed securities because it enables them to make a profit when they make the loan to you and a profit when they sell the loans; it also enables them to free up their money again, so they can make more loans and more money, and it allows them to get the risk that you will not repay your loan off of their own books by passing that risk on to a new owner of your loan. Sometimes when Fannie and Freddie buy home mortgage loans from banks, they even pay the banks to continue servicing those loans. Servicing includes collecting mortgage payments, making sure taxes and insurances are paid, and taking steps if a loan goes into default or foreclosure. The fees paid for servicing mortgage loans are significant, making these "mortgage servicing rights" a valuable asset.

One problem, though, is that when investors (many of whom are foreign, including foreign governments and banks) buy loans from or loans backed by Fannie and Freddie, they have come to expect that if the loans default, Fannie and Freddie (i.e., America's government using your tax dollars) will make good on the loans. This unofficial understanding has come to be known as an *implicit guarantee.*

Because Fannie and Freddie are involved in most home mortgage loans in the new economy and because banks need Fannie and Freddie in order to make more money, Fannie and Freddie have important clout when it comes to getting banks to agree to new rules and reforms like Making Home Affordable. Also important, banks invest time and money setting up systems and procedures for the Fannie- and Freddie-related programs; if the banks can see that the programs work, and since the systems are set up anyway, the banks tend to be open to offering similar programs (called *proprietary* or *private* programs) for mortgage loans that don't involve Fannie or Freddie. So, even if your own home mortgage loan is not owned or insured by Fannie or Freddie, your bank most likely offers triage programs similar to and even building on those offered under Making Home Affordable (for example, "cash for keys," where banks actually pay you money to move out, or "lease for deed," where banks own your home and let you stay there as a renter, all covered in Chapter

5). Making Home Affordable and government-related programs like it have, in essence, served as a "model" for the banks' own proprietary foreclosure triage programs.

In fact, the role of Fannie Mae and Freddie Mac has been so important (in both positive and not-so-positive ways) that they are a focus of both short-term and long-term new rules and reforms.

The Broad-Stroke Themes of New Longer-Term Rules and Reforms

Longer-term rules and reforms are broadly focused on the three main industries said by Washington to have caused the housing bubble, foreclosures, and the Great Recession, necessitating the bailout, namely: front-line real estate and finance-related companies; Fannie Mae, Freddie Mac, and FHA; and Wall Street, banks, and financial institutions.

Front-Line Real Estate and Finance-Related Companies

If you have ever bought, sold, or financed real estate or borrowed money, you know how complicated that process can be and how much you had to rely on professionals, including Realtors, mortgage brokers, appraisers, title insurance companies, closing or settlement services, and the like, in order to navigate the process. Many people have claimed that their experiences were further complicated by professionals they believe may have, either deliberately or inadvertently, done them wrong. For example, there are people who were sold a home mortgage loan (or any one of a variety of loans, credit, or financial services) that they did not fully understand, with terms and conditions that were not accurately disclosed or were entirely inappropriate for them. There are, likewise, plenty of people who have not been able to navigate their mortgage servicers' systems to get help with a modification or have fallen prey to a lawyer who promised to help but then didn't. The new longer-term rules and reforms aimed at front-line real estate and finance-related industries are designed to protect folks like you from potentially being misled this way again, including by Realtors, mortgage brokers, title insurance companies, foreclosure rescue companies, appraisers, and, of course, the now-infamous "robo-signers."

Fannie Mae, Freddie Mac, and FHA

There are dozens of new longer-term rules and reforms still evolving aimed at reducing government's role in housing, including by reining in or eliminating Fannie and Freddie. The numerous suggestions on the table include:

- Restricting Fannie and Freddie's powers, including the total loans they can insure, buy, sell, and hold.

- Changing their entity structure. (Both Fannie and Freddie have obligations to their shareholders to earn as much money as they can, which conflicts with their obligations to the general public to make home mortgage loans available to folks who might not otherwise be able to get such a loan.)

- Adjusting Fannie and Freddie's loan products and how they generate and use revenue.

- Reforming their portfolio, priorities, and practices.

- Clarifying their "implicit guarantee."

On the other hand, you now also know how important it is to the entire American economy, including your own personal financial situation, that folks have an opportunity to own their own homes when possible (in other words, be able to get a sustainable home mortgage loan) and the essential role that Fannie and Freddie have played in this regard. Clearly, the longer-term rules and reforms involving Fannie and Freddie will involve careful balancing and potentially significant unintended consequences you want to keep your eyes open for.

For more on this subject, see the video clip at: www.askshario. com/reform and www.askshario.com/thefalloffannie.

Dodd-Frank Addresses Wall Street

Wall Street and banking products and players have found themselves under a cloud of bailout backlash. Among other new long-term rules and reforms, the Dodd-Frank Wall Street Reform and Consumer Protection Act of 2011 directly addresses Wall Street, banks, and other financial institutions on multiple levels. The impact on you from many of these new rules and reforms will be indirect but no less significant over time. Dodd-Frank is by far the biggest deal out of Washington, not just now, but *ever*! Literally. At 2,300 pages, tree huggers no doubt also consider Dodd-Frank a biggie, too.

As its name suggests, Washington's official stated purpose for Dodd-Frank is to try to *reform* practices on Wall Street (and elsewhere) and *protect* consumers like you. Congress chose three broad themes for Dodd-Frank:

1. First, Dodd-Frank tries to provide strict standards and supervision to protect the economy, investors, and you, and end taxpayer-funded bailouts.

2. Second, the law tries to provide an advance-warning system of future bubbles and crises.

3. Third, Dodd-Frank tries to improve the regulatory agencies that are supposed to be watching out for you by reorganizing Washington's regulators and giving them new powers and rules. There are new rules covering executive compensation and corporate governance and new rules designed to eliminate some of the loopholes blamed for causing the 2008 crises.

As you read this book, you will understand how many of the sections in Dodd-Frank are going to impact you and America, both directly and indirectly. For example, Section 13, the "Pay It Back Act," attempts to limit further increases in America's debt, a topic that indeed impacts you (as you learned earlier in this chapter), albeit indirectly. And given that everyone's financial situation is different, some of the sections in Dodd-Frank will impact some people more or less than others. But for your purposes now, the sections of the law that will likely impact most folks, including you, most clearly and directly are Section 10, which covers the New Consumer Financial Protection Bureau; Section 12, which covers your access to fair loans and credit; and Section 14, which covers home mortgage loans and homeownership for Americans like you. Each will be covered in more detail shortly.

Thanks to Dodd-Frank, you and your fellow Americans are living in historic times. Maybe you've heard that the rules and reforms enacted following (and responding to) the Great Depression brought about some of the biggest changes in the history of our country. The new long-term rules and reforms included in Dodd-Frank and other legislation and programs will likewise have tremendous impacts on you, the country, and future generations!

An Expensive Solution

The Government Accountability Office estimates that implementing Dodd-Frank will require more than 2,600 new regulatory staffers at a cost to the federal government of almost $3 billion. Because six of the eleven agencies responsible for implementing the new rules and reforms get funding, in whole or in part, from assessments levied on the organizations they oversee, a large part of this cost will also be borne by banks and financial service companies. Those companies will, in turn, likely pass these costs on to you, their customers.

Institutions subject to the new rules and refoms have incurred costs of over $2 billion in reporting and paperwork in just the first year, before most of the new provisions have even taken effect. By some estimates, Dodd-Frank resulted in almost 20 million hours of paperwork and compliance in its first year. On top of the costs it will add for businesses, the Congressional Budget Office estimates that, over the next ten years, Dodd-Frank will take $27 billion directly from America's economy to pay for new fees and assessments and reduce the combined profits of twenty-three large financial services companies by about $22 billion annually. By one count, Dodd-Frank requires that regulators create 243 new rules, conduct 67 studies, and issue 22 periodic reports! Dodd-Frank compliance costs for businesses will inevitably be passed along to consumers, either through higher charges elsewhere or reduced services. Likewise, restrictions on the ability of businesses to earn a profit in certain areas will cause them to simply find other areas where they can make a profit. For example, some of the country's biggest banks lost billions as a result of new rules prohibiting various fees, but many have recovered that loss by increasing profits on new mortgage loans since banks have been able to borrow at such low rates and pass along some, but not all, of the savings to folks like you. One thing is for sure: These new rules and reforms are expensive.

State-Level Rules and Reforms

If you or someone you know has ever had a parking ticket or been cited at your home for a building code enforcement violation, you know good and well that the rules and reforms everybody must live by don't come only from America's federal government in Washington, D.C. Each state has its own laws, codes, regulations, programs, initiatives, and statutes, too. Homing in even closer to your home and life, each and every county, city, and town also has its own rules. Just as America's federal government in Washington responded to the Great Recession with a tsunami of new rules and reforms, the various state and local lenders throughout America also responded with a slew of new rules, reforms, and initiatives. It goes without saying that this book cannot possibly cover all of these reforms at all of these levels, so instead, resources to help you find and use the ones that matter to you are provided in the online Appendix. Changes in your state's laws, in particular, are well worth considering as you embark on your own personal financial fresh start. Especially if you live in what have come to be called the "harder hit states," such as Nevada, Arizona, Florida, and California, taking advantage of new resources available to you and being aware of future pitfalls is important. More information specific to the harder hit states is included in the online Appendix, so if you live in one of them, pay especially close attention.

Business Pressures, Negative Press, Lawsuits, and Investigations

What the new rules and reforms don't cover or can't fix, then lawsuits, negative publicity, and good old-fashioned business pressures, including drops in corporate earnings and stock valuations, just might.

Trillions of dollars are still at stake in the litany of lawsuits and other threats to stock values in play.

The same holds true for the multitude of regulatory investigations. In addition to the negative publicity and the cost of investigations to private companies, there is, of course, the fear of fines, penalties, and potentially being shut down or even thrown in jail! There have been a multitude of civil investigations, including the "robo-signer" scandal under investigation for well over a year, which finally culminated when America's biggest banks and attorney generals from virtually every state entered a settlement agreement in 2012. Some of these lawsuits, settlements, and investigations are actually resulting in pools of money being set aside for the benefit of folks who may have been improperly denied a foreclosure alternative or wrongly foreclosed. If you believe you may be one of them, more details are covered in the online Appendix.

What's Next For You?

Impacts from both the short- and longer-term new rules and reforms are unfolding around you even as you read this book. As they continue to be written and implemented, it behooves you to keep your eyes wide open for increasing government costs; decreasing government services; and more new fees and changes from banks, credit companies, and other affected businesses—specific examples of which will be covered for you in the coming chapters. You will likely feel the impact from these changes in your banking, your borrowing, your credit, your debt, your saving, your investing, your retirement, your education and employment, your homeownership decisions, and many other areas of your financial life. There will likewise be an opportunity for those who are informed and looking for it. You are wise to be preparing now. Moving forward you will find ongoing updates in the online Appendix.

For purposes of securing your prosperity, it is far more beneficial that, in demystifying the new rules and reforms, we focus on the reasons and broad-stroke themes rather than on the *specific provisions* themselves. Your goal now is to use the five steps that follow to pinpoint the exact areas in your own personal fresh start that will be most affected by the new rules and reforms, and to pick among the specific tools, tips, and stategies provided in order to secure your financial prosperity moving forward.

PART TWO

The Five Steps

CHAPTER TWO

Step One:
Adapt Your Banking and Borrowing

- **What Will You Learn from This Chapter?** This chapter will teach you how to use the background you have gained (from the previous chapter) to take advantage of new rules and reforms in your banking and borrowing.

- **How Will This Know-How Help You?** Knowing how to leverage these opportunities in the new economy and incorporating this know-how into your personal fresh start plan will allow you to save money and avoid costly pitfalls in the banking and financial services you use and the borrowing that you do (e.g., with your current and future home mortgage loan, car loan, student loan, small-business loan, and credit cards).

You will be happy to know that, at this point, you are officially up to speed on the overriding reasons why The America Company is in the financial situation that it is in today and the broader-stroke themes of the new rules, reforms, and approaches that America's leaders have decided to take to correct the situation. The goal here in step 1 is for you to now begin *using* the knowledge you've gained for your own financial benefit by crafting and then living your own fresh start plan as quickly as possible.

It may be helpful for you to think about designing your fresh start the way you might view designing a new bedroom for yourself. Everything needs to work well together, but most of all, you need to be comfortable in it. The floor plan you create and all the details and accessories that you choose need to be a source of calm, not stress or anxiety, for you. To succeed, your fresh start needs to be one that you can live with. This chapter, and the chapters that follow, help to train your "eye" for efficiently selecting the opportunities you like (and the pitfalls you would like to avoid) from the new rules and reforms that are most relevant to your own personal fresh start.

Since everybody's financial situation and goals are different, these chapters are formatted to allow you to easily pick and choose, from among the various section topics, those that are priorities to you. Simple self-assessments are included in many sections to enable you to quickly decide which sections will benefit your fresh start the most.

Banking Reform or Musical Chairs?

Chapter 1 discussed, in broad-stroke terms, rules and reforms in the banking industry, including what is commonly known as the Dodd-Frank legislation. One result of some of these new banking rules and reforms is that banking, financial services, and borrowing may cost

Self-Assessment: Financial Services and Your Fresh Start

How do the Volcker Rule (explained shortly) and other new banking and financial service rules and reforms relate to your own fresh start and what can you do to protect yourself? This self-assessment will help you to identify the banking and financial services that should be on your fresh start radar screen.

	YES	NO
Do you have a checking account?	☐	☐
Do you have a savings account?	☐	☐
Do you have a bank credit or debit card?	☐	☐
Do you have a financial institution CD or investment account?	☐	☐
Do you receive other financial services from a bank?	☐	☐
Are there other financial services, offered by financial institutions, that you can benefit from?	☐	☐

If you answered Yes to any of these questions, the new banking and financial services rules and reforms will impact your own banking and borrowing.

you more money in the new economy. For example, a section of the Dodd-Frank Act known as the Volcker Rule sought to restrict banks from making certain kinds of risky investments, prohibit banks from owning or investing in hedge funds or private equity funds, limit the liabilities banks could hold, and ban conflict of interest trading by banks—all consistent with the broad-stroke themes of the new long-term rules and reforms you learned about in Chapter 1. The proposal underwent many changes in order to get passed. For example, proprietary trading in certain Treasury bonds and municipal bonds was eventually allowed. Still, the final proposed rule was heavily criticized: Banks considered it too costly to implement, and reform advocates claimed it was too weak and laden with loopholes.

But let's face it, banks are in business to make money (and in fact have obligations to their shareholders, just like other companies, to do so). So if America's government, through the Volcker Rule or other new reforms, tells banks that they can't make money one way, they're going to find other ways to make up for it. The $5 swipe fee that Bank of America tried to introduce in 2012, and others like it, are nothing more than new bank fees designed to make up for revenue the banks lost because of the new rules and reforms. And the $5 swipe fee is only the beginning. Banks have earned more than $24 billion in the past year on new overdraft and other fees! For example, thanks in part to Dodd-Frank, an increasing number of banks are either eliminating free checking accounts or offering them subject to a litany of conditions. (Generally, in order for your bank to give you a free checking account in the new economy, you will need to have a broader relationship with your bank that generates a certain level of profit; in other words, by the time the bank thinks that you've earned a free checking account, that checking account is not actually free after all!)

In addition to becoming more costly, notwithstanding all of the effort to simplify services for average consumers, some banking and financial services may actually become more complicated, too. The new rules governing the opt-in overdraft services explained for you in the One-Minute Mentor below is one example.

To avoid the pitfalls caused by the new rules and reforms, your fresh start strategy can simply incorporate *shopping* for all bank and financial services, just as you might shop the prices you are charged for a manicure or a personal trainer. Tips for avoiding new bank and financial service fees are provided for you in the next section, or check out the online video at www.askshario.com/bankfees.

Fresh Start Tips for Avoiding New Bank Fees

Here are some of the ways you can avoid the new bank fees that emerged from America's well-intended but costly new rules and reforms.

Think

Put some thought into the banking and financial services you need and drill down a bit into how you actually use each of these services. For example, many banks now offer several different checking account options. It behooves you to consider your actual usage in order to ensure that you are not paying for services that you will not use.

Compare

Compare at least three different banks and the details on the services that you need. These details typically fall into two buckets: fees and requirements. More specifically, what are the fees each bank charges for various services, and what are the requirements you have to meet to qualify for those fees? Some banks require that you have direct deposit, maintain a minimum balance (be aware that the trend in the

One-Minute Mentor: Have You Opted In?

The new banking rules and reforms have essentially bifurcated bank overdraft fees. In the new economy, your bank will cover your overdrafts and charge you overdraft fees for doing so only if you "opt in" for that service. If you "opt out," your bank will not cover your overdrafts, but you also will not be charged overdraft fees. Understanding which types of accounts you need to opt in to or out of under the new rules and reforms has become more important than ever before, since the easiest way to avoid paying overdraft fees in the new economy is to simply not opt in.

But here's where the new rules can get a little bit tricky, especially if you're not "in the know." Under the new rules, this opt-in option *is* required before your financial institution can charge you an overdraft fee for single debit card purchases and ATM withdrawals. But it *is not* required that you first opt in for your financial institution to charge you an overdraft fee for overdrafts involving checks, preauthorized electronic payments, or recurring debit card charges! What the heck, right?

new economy is toward increasing the minimum required balance and requiring you to pay an even higher fee if your account balance accidentally slips below it), have multiple accounts at the bank, and pay your bills online in order to avoid additional fees (including additional "per item" fees, for example, 25 cents per check after the tenth check you write in a month). Also ask about program details like a maximum number of overdraft charges per day and low dollar amounts for which the bank won't charge an overdraft fee.

General Strategies

Depending on the bank and financial services you need, it may make sense for you to avoid paying certain fees by switching to a smaller bank or credit union or even to an online bank. Fees can also be sometimes avoided by consolidating accounts and credit cards, or by switching to less expensive banking service (for example, away from a premium account to a more basic checking account and credit card). It may also be worthwhile to look specifically for banks and banking services to which the new rules don't apply; two examples are smaller banks with less than $10 billion in assets, which are exempt from many of the new rules and reforms, and certain services that are exempt from the "Durbin Amendment," which reduced how much banks could charge merchants for debit card swipe fees, and, by way of unintended consequences, resulted in those same banks adding other new fees to replace that lost income.

Rewards

In addition to seeking new sources of revenue, some banks and financial service companies are aggressively cutting expenses. If you use your bank or credit card company's reward program, keep an eye out for signs that the reward program may change or even be phased out; you obviously want to be able to use your rewards before you risk losing them. More tools and tips to help you take the fullest advantage of loyalty and rewards program opportunities are provided later in this book.

Overdraft Fees

If you are prone to bank overdrafts, keep a cushion in your account if you want to avoid paying those big new overdraft fees. (The majority of those fees are due to under $20 in overdrafts!) Try tracking your spending manually, using an old-fashioned paper register; that way there's no need to log onto your computer each time you need to spend money. Pay your bills manually, too (auto-payments are among the leading causes of account overdrafts). If you don't already do so, try using direct deposit so that there are no holds on the money you deposit at the bank, your money is available for you right away, and you are less likely to overdraw your bank account. Consider linking one or more of your bank accounts together if the fee for doing so will be less than the overdraft fees. Avoid joint bank accounts with your spouse (joint accounts significantly increase the chances that one of you will overdraw your bank account). If you do become overdrawn, be sure to pay any overdraft fees quickly in order to avoid being charged even more fees for the same original offense. Under the new rules and reforms, certain new tiered overdraft fee structures can actually translate to even higher overdraft fees the more times you become overdrawn. If you've been prone to overdraft fees in the past, consider all of these proven strategies because they'll help you avoid those costly fees in your banking and borrowing fresh start!

ATM Fees

You will be charged more for using ATMs that do not belong to your own bank. It is always wise to plan your ATM visits and cash needs in advance to avoid using another bank's ATM machines.

Rinse, Wash, Repeat

Like most other businesses, banks innovate, especially when it comes to the potential types of new fees they can charge, even under the new rules and reforms. These innovations are never-ending. It's wise to periodically revisit the financial services you use and how much they cost in order to ensure that you pay the very least amount possible.

They Want You. They Really Want You.

Don't be surprised if your mailbox seems to be filled with more and more "love letters" from your bank and financial service providers as the new economy moves forward and as these institutions strive to comply with the new rules and reforms designed to protect you (and cover their own butts). Reading that microscopic-size print in the letters your credit card company, bank, and other financial service providers send you is an important part of your banking and borrowing fresh start.

Navigating Shrinking Low-Cost Loan and Credit Availability

Much has been written on the subject of using credit. If you're self-disciplined, credit can be a wonderful way to leverage your money, including earning loyalty points, frequent flier miles, and the like. On the opposite end of that spectrum are folks whose credit abuse can be likened to any other addiction that, left unchecked, can easily lead to debt overdose and financial demise. But that's nothing you don't already know. What has *changed* (and has not been much written about, until now) is that access to cost-efficient credit will be more difficult and more costly for many people than it has ever been before. And that's because of the new lending standards and supervision for banks and other financial institutions, which have been instituted by the new rules and reforms, including Dodd-Frank.

So what does the shrinking availability of low-cost credit mean to you? First, if you are carrying a balance for which the interest rate may increase, your prudent fresh start plan includes a method for eventually converting that debt to a more predictable fixed interest rate. If you've historically counted on being able to roll balances over when your interest rate goes up, don't count on being able to do that now! Second, if you have relied on the use of credit to help you pay for essentials in the past, you may find that it is increasingly difficult to do—so incorporating a more balanced budget in your fresh start may be appropriate. Millions of folks were caught unprepared following the bailout when, without any warning, banks across America cut off borrowers' lines of credit (which the banks were legally allowed to do, but no one ever thought they would). Now that you know about this potential pitfall, it just makes sense to avoid it!

Specific-Purpose Borrowing and Your Fresh Start

You know now that, depending on your personal situation, borrowing in general may be more difficult and costly for you in the new economy. Interest on borrowing, including on car loans, student loans, small-business loans, home mortgage loans, and even credit cards is already the highest single consolidated expense most Americans pay each month. One reason is that, as a coping mechanism to get comfortable accumulating so much personal debt, average Americans have learned to focus on the affordability of the amount of a monthly *payment,* rather than the total dollar amount that the loan or credit is actually costing (in the form of interest and other fees) or the total amount that the aggregate payments will cost over time until they're paid off—a rather short-sighted outlook on long-term financial prosperity!

Self-Assessment: Shrinking Low-Cost Loan and Credit Availability and Your Fresh Start

The full impact that the new rules and reforms, and the resulting shrinking availability of low-cost credit, will have on your personal prosperity depends on how much credit you use and how you use it. This simple self-assessment will help you gauge the impact of the new rules on your own finances.

	YES	NO
Do you have or need (now or in the near future) a car loan?	☐	☐
Do you have or need (now or in the near future) a student loan?	☐	☐
Do you have or need (now or in the near future) a business loan?	☐	☐
Do you have or need (now or in the near future) a home mortgage?	☐	☐
Do you have or need more than one loan on your home?	☐	☐
Do you pay for nonessentials with a credit card?	☐	☐
Do you pay for essentials with a credit card?	☐	☐
Do you carry a balance on your credit cards?	☐	☐
If so, is the balance more than 10 percent of your annual income?	☐	☐
If so, have you carried a balance for more than five years?	☐	☐

If you answered Yes to any of these questions, shrinking credit availability due to the new rules, reforms, and economy may impact you—a factor to consider in your banking and borrowing fresh start plan.

Fortunately, there are strategies that you can include in your fresh start banking and borrowing to access the best possible borrowing opportunities should you need them. The Self-Assessment: Shrinking Low-Cost Loan and Credit Availability and Your Fresh Start quickly identifies which of the different types of borrowing are relevant to your own fresh start. Now we want to look at each of them in more detail. Much has been written about shopping for car loans, student loans, business loans, credit cards, and home mortgage loans in general. Unlike general discussions on these topics, the focus of the discussions that follow is specifically on how the new rules and reforms impact these different types of borrowing and your own personal financial situation moving forward.

Home Mortgage Loan Rules and Reforms in the New Economy

Thanks to the new rules and reforms, the home mortgage loan industry is now more highly and uniformly regulated. One result is that folks who may have been taken advantage of before and paid more for their loans now pay what everyone else pays—but everyone else pays more.

Several provisions addressing home mortgage loans are included in the Dodd-Frank Act and other legislation. Perhaps the most widely debated mortgage-related provision is the Qualified Mortgage and Qualified Residential Mortgage (QRM) rule, which is going to be explained shortly. In addition, Dodd-Frank specifies other "minimum standards for mortgages" and introduces the concept of "ability to pay," essentially requiring mortgage loan originators to now confirm that a borrower is able to repay a home mortgage loan before making that loan to the borrower. Yet another section of the Dodd-Frank Act covers "high-cost mortgages," quickly explained for you in the next sidebar.

Why the New Laws Matter

So why do these and other new rules and reforms like them matter to you? Well, earlier you learned that banks prefer to sell the mortgage loans they make so that they can 1) earn a profit on that sale (and as an added bonus get the risk that the borrower will default off of their own books) and 2) loan the money out again and earn more profit. The idea behind the new Qualified Mortgage and QRM rules is that by requiring banks to keep a stake in the home mortgage loans they make (in other words, if the loans default, the banks will have a loss, too), the rules will force banks to be more careful about making risky home mortgage loans (which, you will recall, is a significant broad-stroke theme of the new rules and reforms). But right off the top that means that the 5 percent stake the banks will have to keep

One-Minute Mentor: What Is a High-Cost Mortgage?

Under the new rules and reforms, this term is defined as (at least tentatively) a consumer credit loan secured by a consumer's home. It covers credit transactions if the interest rate is 6.5 percent above the prime rate; subordinated loans (e.g., a second mortgage) if the interest rate is 8.5 percent above the prime rate; loans under $20,000 with total points and fees over 8 percent or $1,000; loans over $20,000 with total points and fees over 6 percent; and loans with the fees and points that may be collected more than thirty-six months later. As you now know, if and when this definition of high-cost mortgage changes, so will your ability to access this type of loan.

Self-Assessment: New Residential Mortgage Rules and Your Fresh Start

Shrinking and more costly borrowing is especially poignant in the case of home mortgage loans. You now know that the broad-stroke themes for both the new short- and long-term rules and reforms focused heavily on home mortgage loan reform. The question is, how will the reforms impact you? This self-assessment will help you begin to answer that question.

	YES	NO
Do you own a home, have a mortgage, and plan to refinance your mortgage?	☐	☐
Do you own a home, not have a mortgage, and plan to get a mortgage?	☐	☐
Do you plan to buy a home with financing?	☐	☐
Do you plan to buy any other type of real estate?	☐	☐

If you answered Yes to any of the above questions, the new mortgage rules will impact your borrowing fresh start.

will no longer be money available for making new home mortgage loans to folks like you. Perhaps even more significant to you is the fact that banks will prefer to make loans that are considered qualified residential mortgages, so they do not have to retain that 5 percent stake. What that means to you is that loans that fall under the definition of a QRM will be easier and cheaper for you to get than loans that do not. Banks that make home mortgage loans falling under the definition of a QRM and abiding by the "ability to pay" rules benefit from certain "safe harbor" laws in case the borrower defaults on the loan and the bank needs to foreclose. Again, it goes without saying that banks will prefer to make loans to you that fall within this safe harbor—and loans that do not are bound to be more expensive, if not impossible, for you to get. The new rules and reforms regarding "requirements to existing residential mortgages" prohibit balloon payments and prepayment penalties. The definition for "high-cost mortgages" is important, too, because these loans are now subject to even further new requirements. For example, for you to get a high-cost mortgage in the new economy, you will first have to receive pre-loan counseling from a certified counselor, once again impacting the availability and cost of different types of home mortgage loans.

There is no doubt that provisions like these (and many others included in the new rules and reforms) make lending less risky for banks, investors, and even borrowers, as is intended by the broad-stroke themes of the new rules and reforms, including Dodd-Frank. For example, potentially requiring as much as a 20 percent down payment from borrowers like you who *do* qualify in order for a mortgage loan to fall into the important qualified residential mortgage category will make mortgage loans less risky for investors, since folks are much less likely to default on their home mortgage loan if they stand to lose a 20 percent investment. But you've learned about unintended consequences and this one's a whopper: Some experts believe that it will take an average American family fourteen years to save up that 20 percent down payment!

The moral of this particular story is that if you plan to apply for a home mortgage loan, your fresh start strategy should account for these new requirements so that you are prepared and will qualify for the most readily available, least expensive home mortgage loans the banks will prefer to sell you. If you anticipate not being able to do that, there is still a window period for you to take advantage of before some of the new rules and reforms take effect.

Home Mortgage Loan Servicing

Both the new rules and reforms and many of the lawsuit and investigation settlement agreements that servicers entered into translate to a long list of new rules and reforms for mortgage servicers, too. You'll recall that servicers are notoriously accused of botching millions of modifications, short sales, and other foreclosure alternative requests from borrowers. Some of the more significant changes require sizable financial investment from servicers and with that, of course, come unintended consequences for you and your wallet. For example, servicers will now be *required* to provide a "single point" of contact for you to communicate with about questions and concerns surrounding your home mortgage loan, clearly a change for the better. But, when American Express offers a higher-level "concierge-style" service, it charges a higher fee. In other words, it is logical that American Express Platinum cardholders pay more money than regular Green cardholders in order to receive that higher level of service. It is likewise logical that one unintended consequence of "single point of contact" and other new mortgage loan servicing reforms is that implementing and operating under these new reforms will ultimately increase what it costs servicers to provide this newly required, heightened level of mortgage loan servicing to you. Unfortunately, these new servicing reforms do not give you the alternative to opt in or out of this new and improved service. You will pay for it one way or another, whether you want it and use it or not.

Fannie and Freddie—Friend or Foe?

Interestingly, as you learned in Chapter 1, the new rules and reforms do not address what will happen to Fannie and Freddie. Despite the fact that, together with FHA, Fannie and Freddie are involved in the vast majority of America's new residential mortgage loans and an even higher percentage of all securitized home mortgage loans, the new rules and reforms target banks and financial service providers, not the American government's own allegedly risky home mortgage loan businesses. In fact, partly in order to keep mortgages available until the economy and housing bounce back a bit, Fannie and Freddie mortgage loans and borrowers are actually *excluded* from some of the tougher new rules and reforms. In the short term, Fannie and Freddie may continue to be a good source for relatively less expensive, more flexible home mortgage loans. But given that Fannie and Freddie's risk is actually taxpayer money at risk, one unintended consequence is that American taxpayers may arguably end up exposed to even further potential financial loss.

As discussed in Chapter 1, some experts believe the American government's goal should be to reduce Fannie and Freddie's importance in the home mortgage loan industry altogether. But to do so, other banks would have to be encouraged to step in and take over the huge role Fannie and Freddie have played. Another important unintended consequence of exempting Fannie and Freddie from many of the new rules and reforms is that it gives them a gigantic business advantage over other banks—which are the same banks the experts believe need to be encouraged to participate in the home mortgage loan market. Chapter 5 drills down further into home mortgage loan fresh start opportunities in the new economy, including foreclosure alternatives; investing in real estate for a profit; and ways you can know when to buy, sell, or rent.

Car Loans Rules and Reforms in the New Economy

Are you thinking about buying a new or used car in the next few years? Wondering what kind of car loan you'll be able to get under the new rules and reforms? You know that one broad-stroke theme is protecting you from lenders who might otherwise loan you money that the government thinks you might not be able to afford to repay. But what you may not realize is that car loans are the second highest debt for average Americans and, as such, have not gone unnoticed by the crafters of the new rules and reforms. In the new economy, car loans are still accessible to the *prime* car loan borrower. But the credit scores required for the best car loan terms have risen to 720 or even 740 from around 700. If you're an *average* car loan borrower, plan to come up with a 10 percent to 15 percent down payment. And if you're a *subprime* car loan borrower (as about 20 percent of today's car buyers are), you will still be able to find a decent car loan, but be prepared to compromise and work harder to get approved. If your credit score is under 500, you may want to consider riding a bicycle until you can improve it.

On the other hand, the car loan industry has certainly recognized the reality that over 60 percent of Americans now have lower credit scores than they did before the crisis. The good news here is that, if this describes your own situation, you can still access a car loan, but your fresh start plan may need to incorporate higher than usual self-discipline for now. Deep subprime car loan borrowers pay as much as 18 percent interest on car loans. So, once again, the big costs are disproportionately borne by folks on the lower end of the borrowing spectrum, essentially those who can least afford it. You can mitigate this added cost by distinguishing reality (necessary transportation) from illusion (a lifestyle you cannot really afford at the moment). Until you get back on the financial path you want to be on, don't buy into an illusion. Borrow only what you absolutely have to.

Buy the Financing First

Shopping for a car loan as aggressively as you shop for the car itself will save you money. But dealers know that's not what most folks do. Most folks decide in advance what type of car they want. There's relatively little that the salesman has to do to "seal the deal." There's a price on the sticker, which most folks inevitably negotiate down at least a little bit and then feel as if they're getting a good deal. Then the salesman leads the way to meet with the finance guy. That's where your luck runs out and the "sale" actually begins. Inch by inch, dollar by dollar, the aggregate amount that buying the car will actually cost you gets ratcheted up. Some of the increases you're aware of—for example, add-ons you hadn't thought about, but think you want or need, like "undercarriage sealer" or "prepaid maintenance checkups." Other increases in the amount you will ultimately pay for your car are more elusive. Costs tied in to the car loan itself typically fall into that bucket.

In truth, the finance office in a car dealership is, in and of itself, a lucrative profit center. Top dealer revenue sources include fees earned by the dealer by selling customers (like you) car loans, extended warranties, credit insurance (where the insurance company pays off your car loan if you die or become disabled), gap insurance (where the insurance company pays the difference between what your car is worth and what you owe, in case of an accident), and a wide range of aftermarket upgrades, from rust proofing to car alarms to window tinting.

A prudent car loan fresh start puts shopping for the loan, and all those add-ons you think you need (and frankly are sometimes even afraid to not buy), on equal footing with shopping for the car itself. In other words, fall in love with the *financial* piece of your car purchase first! Picture how good a low monthly car payment will feel in comparison to a high one, and how much you will enjoy spending the money you save on something else, or the sense of security that comes with knowing that you will be saving it for a rainy day. This is true particularly in tough times, when you are more likely to be upside down on your trade-in, which is another oftentimes hidden profit margin for the dealer at even further cost to you (more than 20 percent of Americans who bought a new car last year still had an average of almost $4,000 in negative equity on their trade-in!). For more on car loans, check out the online video clips at www.askshario.com/carbuying1 and www.askshario.com/carbuying2.

Fresh Start Tips for Getting a Car Loan

Here are some more fresh start tips for vetting car loans in the new economy and under the new rules and reforms:

- *Bye-Bye Impulse Buys.* Plan ahead for your car purchase. The days of "impulse" buys are long gone.

- *Auto Industry Credit Scores.* Clean up your credit score as much as possible before you do anything else. Find out what credit scores your dealer uses. Some dealers now use the "FICO Auto Industry Option" score, based on car-specific factors such as your car buying history, car payment history, and repossessions. If you are a first-time buyer or have no previous car loans on your credit report, you may score low on the Auto Industry Option score, even if you have an excellent FICO score, so ask ahead of time.

- *Play It Safe.* To be safe, your total car costs should not exceed 15 percent to 20 percent of your take-home pay.

- *MSRP "Sticker" Price vs. Dealer Invoice.* Negotiate up from the dealer invoice instead of down from the sticker price.

- *New vs. Used.* When considering the new-vs.-used car decision, know that used cars may be cheaper and easier to qualify for, but the interest rates on used car loans are higher.

- *Car Loan Sources.* Loaning money for car purchases is big business, so most car manufacturers have their own companies to arrange car loans. But car buyers are often overcharged on average 3 percent on their loans at the dealership. Your own bank may be able to offer you a better rate than most other car loan lenders if you're an existing customer and the bank is already comfortable doing business with you. Credit unions are another wonderful place to look for a car loan. About 90 million Americans are already credit union members, and half of all fixed-term loans given by America's 8,000-plus credit unions are for car purchases!

- *Do Your Homework.* Shop interest rates and car loan terms online so that you're educated going in.

- *Get It in Writing.* If you're getting a car loan, get it approved in writing before you decide on the car. With an approved car loan, you can act like a cash buyer and negotiate harder on price.

- *The Dreaded Down Payment.* In the new economy, almost every borrower (other than perhaps those with the very best credit) will have to make a down payment, or a bigger down payment (about 10 percent bigger) than before, to get good rates. Car loan lenders require down payments in order to make the quality of the car loans on their own books look better. If you're a subprime borrower, plan to save up at least 20 percent to put down on a car. With a 30 percent down payment, you may even qualify for the interest rates now normally reserved for more prime borrowers.

- *Proof of Income.* Be prepared to prove your income and to have the car loan company call your employer to verify that income if you want to get a decent interest rate and car loan terms.

- *Outsmart the Bait and Switch.* Don't assume that you'll get those wonderful advertised car loan interest rates and terms. They're generally for super prime borrowers (who lenders are actually fighting over!). When you do get the real skinny on the car loan you qualify for, focus on the *total* amount of money that buying the car will take out of your pocketbook by the time you pay off the entire loan and not on how much the *monthly* payment alone will cost. Obviously, the longer you take to pay off the loan, the lower the monthly payments will be, but you will wind up paying more for the car. In addition, the amount of your monthly payment will depend on the interest rate and the amount of your down payment.

- *Trade-Ins.* If you're upside down on your trade-in, the dealer may offer you a "stacked loan" that pays off your old car and finances the new one. The problem is, it also puts you way upside down on your new car. Just say "no."

- *Other Costs.* Don't forget to factor in the costs of insurance, fuel, and maintenance when deciding on a car. Bigger cars use more fuel but may cost less for insurance than smaller cars. Older cars may cost less but have more repair costs than a new car with a warranty and typically carry higher interest rate loans.

- *Read Before You Sign.* Take your time. Don't be afraid to ask for a copy of the car loan documents to take home with you so that you can read them in the comfort of your own home, when you're not feeling pressured, and be sure you understand them before you sign them. Remember that losing a car to repossession has an even bigger impact on your ability to earn a living than losing a home!

Student Loan Rules and Reforms in the New Economy

If you're not in the market for a student loan yourself and are thinking that the new rules and reforms surrounding student loans don't really matter to you, think again. Excessive student loan debt impacts your own personal financial situation by slowing America's economic recovery, including the housing market recovery. After all, student loan borrowers sending big payments to their student loan servicers each month can hardly afford to become first-time homebuyers or vibrant consumers in the broader economy (see Figure 2-1).

America's student loan debt now exceeds $1 trillion; defaulted federal student loans already total almost $50 billion; and, as you will learn in Chapter 8, the ability (or inability) of America's next generation to access affordable education and pay their bills has far-reaching implications for everybody.

In part, because federal student loan limits have not kept up with the rising costs of college tuition, the private student loan business has bridged the gap. Private student loans generally come from banks, financial companies, or through the schools themselves. As private student loan businesses extended into this space, borrowers increasingly found private student loans to be more quickly accessible—to the point where, oftentimes, they no longer seek federal student loan alternatives in the first place. The problem is that, historically, private student loan rates and terms have not been regulated and have tended to be more costly; they often lack the more prudent and predictable terms, such as a fixed interest rate and more flexible repayment options (such as discharge, deferment, and forbearance), that the federal student loans allow. And because they're based on credit score, once again, low-income students or those with negative credit histories bear the disproportionate burden of more expensive private student loans. Some say this shift bore similarities to the shift toward subprime mortgage loans, not the least of which includes the fact that America's government and taxpayers are winding up paying the price.

These are among the reasons that the new rules and reforms address student loans and, more specifically, that the new Consumer Financial Protection Bureau (CFPB) has stated it will pay particular attention to regulating student loans.

Figure 2-1. Student loans are increasing faster than other borrowing.

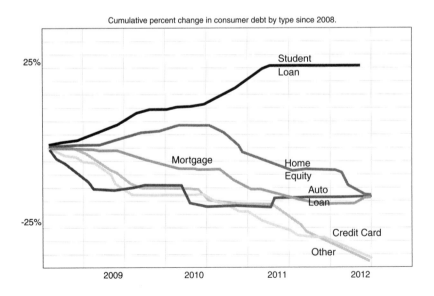

Among other things, the new rules and reforms create a private student loan "ombudsman" at the CFPB to help student loan borrowers with, for example, difficulties making full payments, billing disputes, deferment and forbearance issues, debt collection and credit reporting problems, or simply those confused by advertising or marketing terms. The ombudsman also is charged with developing new student loan recommendations for Congress and other federal government agencies. There are now new disclosures required for private student loans, so the CFPB, together with the Department of Education, has launched an initiative called "Know Before You Owe," which provides a financial aid shopping worksheet, available online, for students. This tool helps folks to better understand their student loans and comparison shop. Some of the new student loan rules and reforms are quickly recapped for you in the next section. Most of these changes became effective with the 2012–2013 school year.

A Sampling of New Student Loan Rules

If your fresh start plan includes a student loan, here are some of the new student loan rules and reforms to which you will want to pay particular attention:

High School Diploma

If you are enrolling in college for the first time, then to be eligible for a new federal student loan you need to have a high school diploma or its equivalent (e.g., a GED certificate showing you've passed the General Educational Development test), or have been home-schooled.

Expected Family Contribution

The lower your expected family contribution, the higher the student's federal student aid eligibility will be. When you complete the Free Application for Federal Student Aid (FAFSA) application, you will receive an expected family contribution, which is the number used to determine your federal student aid eligibility. The previous maximum income of $32,000 has been lowered.

Pell Grant Program

The federal Pell Grant Program has been supplemented with additional funding (both a higher amount of funds available and more students who will be able to qualify for them) and is now available all year round, instead of just in the fall. You're eligible if your expected family contribution is 95 percent or less of the grant. But if you've received a Pell Grant for twelve semesters or its equivalent, then you're not eligible for further grants.

Direct Student Loans

To keep federal student loans accessible and avoid more student loan defaults, the government created the Ensuring Continued Access to Student Loans Act of 2008 and a "direct loan" initiative. As a result, students who were used to going through private lenders to get federal loans now go right to the government. Origination fees on federal loans are now lower (one percent with another 0.5 percent fee rebate available after the loan is disbursed), and direct loans offer a 0.25 percent reduction on interest for borrowers paying by automatic debit.

Subsidized Loans

Subsidized student loans are those for which the borrower is not responsible for the interest if (1) the student is enrolled in college on at least a half-time basis; (2) the loan is in the six-month grace period after the student is no longer enrolled at least half-time; or (3) the loan is in a deferment status. The new rules eliminate the interest subsidy provided during the six-month grace period for subsidized loans if the first disbursement is made by July 1, 2014. If you receive a subsidized student loan during this time, you will be responsible for the interest that accrues while your loan is in the grace period. You do not have to make payments during the grace period but, if you don't, then interest will be added on to the principal amount of your student loan when the grace period ends. This provision does not eliminate the interest subsidy while the borrower is in school or during eligible periods of deferment. If your fresh start plan involves a subsidized student loan, then make sure you keep an eye on the interest rates, because debate on the subject continues. Graduate and professional students are no longer eligible to receive subsidized loans. However, if you are a graduate or professional student, you can still qualify for up to $20,500 in unsubsidized loans each year.

Repayment Incentives

The United States Department of Education no longer offers repayment incentives.

Income-Based Repayment

The government also rolled out a new income-based repayment plan for borrowers who have federal student loans with accrued interest to repay. Instead of calculating eligibility based on the balance of the student loan when the borrower began repaying it, the government now uses the greater of the original student loan balance or the current student loan balance. Former students can consolidate multiple loans into one loan, cap loan payments at 10 percent of their discretionary income, and forgive the balance after twenty years of payments. This changes the prior program that capped repayment at 15 percent of income and allowed forgiveness after twenty-five years.

Married Borrowers

As America's economy continued to drag, the government subsequently made even further new rules and reforms easing student loan repayment. One such new reform calculates income-based repayments for married borrowers with federal student loans by weighing the total student loan debt for the household against total household income; previously, the system did not take into account total household student debt, meaning that married borrowers had to pay up to twice the amount that two single borrowers paid.

More tips for navigating the new student loan rules and reforms can be found in the video clip you'll find at www.askshario.com/studentloans.

Perhaps most important, for purposes of your own fresh start, the question of whether a college education pays off is no longer a no-brainer but instead requires thoughtful planning and consideration. Chapter 8 further discusses the issues of top-paying education and career choices for ensuring your future prosperity in the new economy and whether college is even worth incorporating into your fresh start and spending your money on anymore.

Small Business Loan Rules and Reforms in the New Economy

Even before the new rules and reforms began rolling out, most banks had already pulled back from making small-business loans. In fact, it was not uncommon, following the bailout, to hear of small businesses that seemed to be doing just fine suddenly having their lines of credit yanked, essentially because their bank was concerned about the economy. (Many small business and other types of loan documents contain provisions allowing the bank to stop funding your loan if the bank determines that an "adverse financial change" has occurred.) In the new economy, many banks are still investing time and resources resolving problems and are more reluctant than before to take the risk of making new loans to small businesses—which in truth, thanks in large part to new economic challenges, do indeed tend to be less creditworthy. Even Small Business Administration (SBA) loans, historically a top source for small-business funding, dropped by about a third.

Unfortunately, small businesses have also historically relied more heavily on local community banks for funding. But smaller community banks, in particular, find it more difficult than larger banks to comply with all of the new rules and reforms, simply because they do not have the same financial resources and cannot benefit from the same economies of scale that larger banks enjoy when it comes to absorbing the costs of understanding, gearing up for, and implementing all of the new rules and reforms. In addition, some of the new rules and reforms themselves have a disproportionate impact on smaller community banks simply because of the types of loans smaller community banks tend to have historically made. Small banks (in this context, meaning banks with under $1 billion in total assets) make up only about 10 percent of the banking deposit market, but they make approximately 40 percent of all loans to small businesses. Section 1071 of Dodd-Frank, for example, has gained particular attention in regard to its impact on community banks and small-business lending. Briefly, Section 1071 amends the Equal Credit Opportunity Act to facilitate enforcement by requiring banks to collect and report information made by women- and minority-owned business loan applicants. On the one hand, this particular new rule was intended to ensure that women- and minority-owned businesses are offered loans and terms similar to everyone else, which sounds wonderful. On the other hand, one unintended consequence is that Section 1071 also arguably restricts a bank's flexibility to make more customized types of loans that small-business borrowers tend to need.

Think small-business loans don't matter to you? Think again! Small-business growth in turn spurs broader economic growth, furthering new business development and J-O-B-S. Small businesses employ 80 million Americans. Start-ups with access to $50,000 or more in capital historically have a better chance of keeping their doors open than those without capital. In fact, insufficient access to capital is the number-one reason most small businesses fail and jobs are lost. If you anticipate needing a small-business loan for your own personal fresh start, the following section quickly summarizes a few tips for improving your chances of getting one under the new rules and reforms.

Fresh Start Tips for Getting a Small-Business Loan

Here are some important fresh start tips involving your search for small-business loans.

Find the Right Banks and Bankers

Find three banks and bankers you believe you connect with. Make sure each bank provides the type of small-business loan you think you may need and would consider borrowing. Make sure that each lends to businesses that are the same size and type and are in the same industry as yours (some banks focus their lending on mature small businesses rather than start-ups, for example). It is much simpler to do business with a bank that understands and is comfortable with the risk of lending to a business in your industry.

Invest in Building Relationships

Put time into building a strong relationship with your banker before requesting a small-business loan. Aim to create a relationship where the banker understands your business and is excited and updated periodically on the progress your business is making; as a result, when you begin asking about a small-business loan, your banker already knows you and your business, doesn't have to start at square one in the education process, and can advocate for you inside the bank.

Look Good on Paper

Be prepared to show your banker evidence of your business's strength. Simply put, in order to obtain a loan, businesses need to show that they are making money. Small-business loans based only on business assets are a thing of the past. In the new economy, you will need to show cash flow and profit performance if you want to get a small-business loan. Your current balance sheet, profit-and-loss statement, and a detailed budget clearly reflecting that your business will be making money over the next twenty-four months are all "must haves."

See Your Business from Your Banker's Perspective

Anticipate your banker's concerns. Give her a candid assessment of the risks that you perceive your business faces and how you plan to mitigate these risks. It's important that your banker sees that you recognize your own business's risks and that you have a plan for dealing with them.

Stay Flexible

Plan to remain a bit flexible, including with the amount of money and small-business loan terms that you will accept. If you sense resistance from your banker, offer to reduce the loan amount or agree to some loan terms that your banker might consider less risky for the bank. By doing so you'll build trust so that you can ask for more money and even better loan terms the next time.

If you or someone you know is in need of a small-business loan, not to worry: There is a silver lining to the more acute challenges small businesses seeking loans face under the new rules and reforms in today's new economy. First, America's government, aware of the challenges and the importance of small-business lending, is leveraging the Small Business Administration and lending is on the rise again. For small businesses of any age or size, the SBA offers a variety of loan programs. The SBA website is also a wonderful resource for finding other types of small-business loans, grants, and financing programs that you may be eligible for. Second, thanks in part to opportunities created by the void in small-business lending, and by the low returns investors are earning on investments in general in the new economy, less conventional small-business lending, including micro-lending (see next sidebar), is becoming increasingly popular.

For more about small-business loans in the new economy, check out the online Appendix.

Credit Card Reform Gone Wild

For purposes of your own borrowing fresh start, credit card reform means that banks and credit card companies will be looking even harder for new ways to make money from you. Unfortunately, most credit cardholders have not made that very difficult to do.

Incredibly, more than 30 percent of folks who carry a credit card balance still don't know how much interest they pay, almost 70 percent don't understand their own credit card terms, and over a third say that they are not at all aware of the new credit card rules and reforms. Among the new rules and reforms most relevant to your own borrowing fresh start are those found in the Credit Card Accountability, Responsibility, and Disclosure (CARD) Act. This act amended the Truth in Lending Act to establish more fair and transparent practices relating to the extension of credit, including credit cards, under open-ended consumer credit plans. Here are some of the ways the new rules are intended to protect you.

Micro-Lending Comes to America

Micro-lenders, including nonprofit community organizations, offer loans between $500 and $35,000. Interest rates on micro-loans today can range up to around 14 percent, and loan terms span from a few months to a few years. In addition, many micro-lenders also offer business plan writing programs, marketing training, and other valuable resources to help small-business micro-loan borrowers succeed. In part because of this added value, the default rate for micro-loans is significantly lower than the default rate for traditional small-business bank loans. In fact, the American government earmarked millions in stimulus money for the Small Business Administration's own micro-loan program.

Micro-lending has already proved to be an attractive alternative for millions of Americans who have given up on dismal job prospects and started their own small businesses or are expanding small business they may have started in their spare time. In fact, the number of micro-loans given to small businesses has almost doubled since the bailout.

Interest Rate Increases

Prior to the Credit Card Accountability, Responsibility, and Disclosure Act, it was not uncommon for credit card companies to raise your interest rate (including the interest rate applied to your *existing* credit card balance) with little or no advance warning. In fact, this happened to about 15 percent of credit cardholders each year. The CARD Act prohibits credit card companies from increasing the interest rate on your existing credit card balance unless you have missed two of your credit card payments in a row. Credit card companies are still allowed to increase the interest rate for new purchases you make on your credit cards, but they now have to give you forty-five days advance written notice. If you're not on board with the interest rate increase, you can cancel your credit card during this period or just stop making new charges with it. But, again, the hitch is that you need to actually read those notices.

Late Fees

Before the new CARD Act, there were several ways that you could incur a credit card late fee, and the fees themselves often seemed excessive. Americans were paying more than $900 million a year in credit card fees and penalties on $800 billion in outstanding credit card debt. Under the new rules, your credit card company can't charge you a late fee unless you have at least twenty-one days to pay your credit card bill. Additionally, your credit card bill now has to be due on the same date each month, and as long as your payment is received by 5:00 p.m. on the due date, the credit card company has to consider it as being made on time. Confusion over monthly due dates is said to have resulted in as much as $5 billion in costs every year. Now, if your credit card company does charge you a late fee or other penalty, it has to be "reasonable and proportional" to the term in your credit card agreement that you breached. As you know, when it comes to the use of defined terms in the new rules and reforms, such as "reasonable" and "proportional," the devil is in the details. In this case, the CARD Act includes a "safe harbor" to help define these terms As long as your late fee does not exceed your minimum payment when due and is not more than $25 for your first violation and $35 for your second violation within six months, it will be considered "reasonable and proportional."

Over-Limit Fees

Before the new rules and reforms, your credit card company, much like your bank, had carte blanche to process charges you may have made that were over your credit limit and then charge you an "over-limit fee" for doing so, all without you really knowing what was going on. About 12 percent of credit cardholders wound up paying these fees each year. And even after that, if you didn't pay enough money to bring your balance down so that it was within your approved credit limit, your credit card company would charge you another over-limit fee again each month. Under the new rules and reforms, your credit card company can only charge you an over-limit fee if you specifically "opt in" to allow your credit card company to process these over-limit transactions (and you can revoke your opt-in consent at any time). In addition, any time your credit card company now charges you an over-limit fee, it must remind you, in writing, of your legal right to revoke your opt-in authorization. Credit card companies also can't charge more than one over-limit fee on your bill, and the amount of the over-limit fee itself is subject to the same limitations as other fees and penalties.

Credit Card Statements

Another area of concern addressed by the new rules and reforms is monthly credit card statements, which made it difficult to understand how much your credit card was actually costing you. The new rules and reforms now require that your monthly statements show you how long it will take you to pay off your bill, how much more it will cost you if you only pay the minimum amount each month, the total interest you have paid for the year, and other similar information about how much using your credit card actually costs you. For example, your statements also need to show you how much money you need to pay each month to pay off your credit card bill in three years and how much money you will save doing so, in comparison to only making the minimum payment each month. (Yet, more than half of all credit cardholders still remain unaware that their credit card bill clearly tells them how much to pay each month in order to pay off the balance within three years.) If you are struggling with getting out from underneath big credit card balances, this is a wonderful new tool to incorporate into your fresh start.

It seems the new rules and reforms are working. Following enactment of the new rules, the total fees and penalties paid by folks dropped to under $430 million a year (still a lot of dough wasted for basically nothing!) and the average late fee dropped to $23. In addition, only about 2 percent of cardholders are now seeing interest rates increase on their existing credit cards in this manner. And over-limit fees are now more or less nonexistent.

But you know good and well that when credit card companies lose one source of revenue they will eventually replace it with another. For example, since the new rules and reforms took effect, six of the nine biggest credit card companies have increased the amount of the minimum monthly payment they charge you, presumably so they can charge you higher late fees and still be in compliance under the safe harbor just discussed as contained in the new rules. And five of the top nine credit card companies have increased, or plan to increase, the interest rates on new purchases if you are late on your credit card payments; several credit card companies have specifically reserved the right to increase your credit card interest rate if you are even a single day late in making your credit card payments. The moral of this story is, now more than ever before, don't be late on your credit card payments.

Unintended Consequences of the Credit Card Accountability, Responsibility, and Disclosure Act

You know that new rules and reforms can have unintended consequences. So what are some of the unintended consequences of the CARD Act? Perhaps the most significant thus far is that, notwithstanding that interest rates in general are at all-time lows, the average interest rates you are charged by credit card companies have increased by more than 2 percent, translating to an additional cost to credit cardholders of almost $17 billion a year! The cost of transferring your credit card balance is also up. Before the new rules and reforms, almost a third of all credit card companies had a maximum fee they would charge you for transferring balances; now, virtually all companies charge a percentage of the balance amount transferred, and the average amount of fees actually charged to transfer balances since the new rules took effect has risen by almost 1.5 percent.

And again it is folks who can least afford it who are bearing the brunt of this new burden. If you have good credit, you may only be paying one percent to 2 percent more today. But if you are at the lower end of the credit score spectrum, you may be paying as much as 3 percent or 4 percent more. While this increase may be due, in part, to the lower credit scores so many folks have nowadays, there is little doubt that it is also partly an effort by the credit card companies to make up for some of the revenue they have lost, thanks to the new rules and reforms. So, in essence, the new rules and reforms may indeed protect credit cardholders who had been victims of late fees and over-limit fees and the like, but that protection has come at higher costs to everyone.

Having this new knowledge is half of your fresh start challenge. The challenge ends, the rubber hits the road, and the fresh start begins when you start to use this knowledge to achieve your own financial prosperity. Thirty-one percent of folks who recall seeing the information required by the new rules and reforms on their credit card bill say that this new information has prompted them to increase the monthly credit card payments they make and reduce their overall credit card use.

Fresh Start Tips for Credit Cards

Since everybody's credit and debit card situation is different, here are some of the more universal tools to help you manage your own credit card fresh start in the new economy.

Take Advantage of Introductory Rates

The new Credit Card Accountability, Responsibility, and Disclosure Act requires credit card companies to keep introductory rates in place for at least six months, as long as you pay on time. Take advantage of this new opportunity by using zero percent interest or low introductory interest rates to your fresh start benefit. During that introductory period, put your monthly payments toward your balance and get it paid down or even paid off!

Evaluate Balance-Transfer Opportunities

If you're taking advantage of a balance-transfer offer, make sure you understand the fees and how the transfer affects your credit score. Do your homework and take advantage of the opportunity offered by online credit score recalculators. For example, calculate whether you should close out your old credit cards after you transfer or pay off the balances. On the one hand, your credit score may take a small hit when a new credit card issuer checks it. But, on the other hand, having additional credit at your disposal may improve your score over time (credit score fresh start tips are covered in detail in the next chapter). The trick is not to run up another new balance on that old card. Instead, use it a little bit every few months and pay it off in full just to keep it open.

Hope for the Best, but Plan for the Worst

If you *have* to carry a balance on a credit card, look for the lowest interest rate and, if possible, convert balances to a more predictable fixed interest rate. Include the "worst-case" scenario monthly payment in your fresh start budget. Don't be fooled by bells and whistles. You're probably better off with a lower rate than a rewards card, since what you pay in interest may exceed what you make in rewards.

Avoid Late Pays (They Are Worse Than Ever)

Making credit card payments on time under the new rules and reforms is essential if you want to avoid penalty fees, but even more important to avoid those penalty interest rate hikes. Some credit card companies even put your rewards at risk if you pay late. You may stop accruing rewards, lose the rewards you've already accumulated, or get charged a fee to regain them. And of course, paying late can lower your credit score.

Invest Time Finding Benefits

In addition to avoiding credit card penalty pitfalls under the new rules and reforms, assuming you can get the best interest rate, too, take advantage of the opportunities that exist as well. Everyone knows about miles, points, cash back, and other credit card rewards. However, some credit cards offer other perks that can be just as valuable. They include extended warranties (meaning that you don't have to spend your own money to extend the warranty on items you buy with your credit card); traveler's services, such as roadside assistance, travel insurance, and lost-baggage coverage; theft, breakage, and loss protection; or purchase protection (meaning if you find the same item for a lower price, the credit card company will match it). The easiest way to find out what's available is to check online resources and call your current credit card company and ask. And again, read those inserts that come with your bill. They will alert you to special promotions and to changes in the programs.

The Bottom Line

Do the new rules and reforms in banking and borrowing really make these aspects of your financial life less costly and more transparent, or is the whole thing just a game of musical chairs? There's little doubt that, for many folks, the new rules and reforms mean less access to low-cost loans and credit. In essence, everybody is paying more so that those at the subprime end of the banking and borrowing spectrum can be treated more equally. Your home loan, student loan, car loan, small-business loan, even your credit cards are all impacted by the new rules and reforms. Now more than ever, reading the fine print, particularly in the mail from your loan and credit card providers, is a must if you want to protect yourself from higher fees. At the end of the day, taking ownership of your own banking and borrowing behaviors is unavoidable, and now you're well prepared to do just that!

Now it's on to step 2, where you will learn how the new rules and reforms affect your efforts to clean up (or perhaps simply just improve) your credit and manage your debt in the new economy.

CHAPTER THREE

Step Two:
Fix Your Credit and Debt

- **What Will You Learn from This Chapter?** This chapter will teach you some super-easy ways to apply the knowledge that you now have about the new rules, reforms, and economy to your own personal credit and debt fresh start.

- **How Will This Know-How Help You?** Knowledge delivered in this chapter allows you to take advantage of opportunities and avoid pitfalls under the new rules and reforms to get your debt under control, clean up your credit, and ensure that you use both to your fullest benefit moving forward.

If you're fortunate enough to have zero debt and perfect credit, feel free to skip the sections in this chapter that do not apply to your own personal situation. But if you're facing debt or credit challenges, stabilizing these facets of your financial life is essential so that you can move forward without the risk of either becoming a fresh start obstacle. Depending on your specific credit and debt situation, your fresh start may involve navigating aggressive collections agencies, working with debt managers and credit counselors, or even considering bankruptcy; you'll also want proven strategies for repairing or perhaps simply just improving your credit score and ensuring a balanced budget moving forward. All of these options will be quickly covered for you in this chapter.

Life, Liberty, and the Pursuit of a Good Credit Score

Monitoring and managing your credit score is a vital part of managing your credit and debt.

Thanks to the Great Recession, more than 43 million Americans now have severe credit blemishes, including Fair Isaac Credit Organization (FICO) credit scores under 620. If you're one of them, this next section includes everything you need to know to fresh start your FICO score.

Now an icon in the credit reporting industry, the Fair, Isaac and Company was formed in 1956; renamed the Fair Isaac Corporation in 2003; and renamed again in 2009, becoming FICO. Each individual FICO score actually has three credit scores in it because the three national credit bureaus in America—Experian, Equifax, and TransUnion—each have their own database. The data about an individual consumer varies from bureau to bureau, as each credit reporting agency gathers information from various and sometimes different providers. Under the new rules and reforms, you can get your own credit report for free once a year, and you can buy two of your three FICO scores anytime you want at www.myFICO.com (one of the three credit bureaus, Experian, no longer sells FICO scores to consumers). Checking your own credit report as you embark on your financial fresh start won't affect your score, as long as you order your credit report directly from the credit reporting agency or through an organization authorized to provide credit reports to consumers.

If you've taken a credit hit and your own credit score happens to be lower today than it was a few years ago, believe it or not, you're in luck. Low credit scores are viewed with less skepticism in the new economy than ever before. Nevertheless, those low numbers will still cost you higher dollars when it comes to services that base the fees they charge you on your credit score. If you're not exactly sure where you fall on the credit score spectrum, check out this quick self-assessment.

Self-Assessment: Where Do You Rank on the Credit Score Spectrum?

Super prime: 740 to 850

Prime: 680 to 739

Nonprime: 620 to 679

Subprime: 550 to 619

Deep Subprime: 300 to 550

The Fair Credit Reporting Act

Because your credit score has grown to be so important, the new Consumer Financial Protection Bureau is regulating credit bureaus especially carefully under the new rules and reforms, including by enforcing the federal Fair Credit Reporting Act.

The purpose of the Fair Credit Reporting Act (FCRA) is to stipulate who can and cannot get a copy of your credit report and under what circumstances, and to promote accuracy, fairness, and information privacy in consumer reporting agencies and the way your credit information is shared and used. Companies that supply your credit information to consumer credit reporting agencies have to follow specific credit reporting rules.

Among other things, FCRA provides that you must be told if information in your file has been used against you. The act also says that you have the right to know what is in your credit file and to ask for your own credit score. More particularly, you are entitled to a free copy if anyone has taken adverse action against you because of information contained in your credit report, if you are the victim of identity theft and place a fraud alert in your file, if your file contains inaccurate information as a result of fraud, and if you are on public assistance and are unemployed but expect to apply for employment within sixty days. If there is incomplete or inaccurate information in your file, you have the right to dispute that information in your file, and agencies must correct or delete inaccurate, incomplete, or unverifiable information. Also, agencies may not report outdated negative information.

The Fair Credit Reporting Act also limits access to your file by third parties, and your consent is required in order for your report to be provided to your employer. You can also limit the "prescreened" offers of credit and insurance you get based on information in your credit report. Unsolicited prescreened offers for credit and insurance must include a toll-free phone number you can call if you wish to remove your name from the lists these offers come from (to opt out, simply call 1-888-5-OPTOUT); you can seek damages from violators.

Improving Your Credit Score

The good news is that a badly battered credit score isn't a life sentence. If you do nothing at all, your credit score will recover on its own in seven to ten years. The even better news is that there are things you can do to resuscitate your credit score even faster if you don't want to wait. Improving your credit score is an important cornerstone of almost any fresh start plan. The number of variables that play into an individual score make it impossible to say whether any one particular action will increase a given score by a certain number of points. But this section will fill you in on some good guidelines.

One-Minute Mentor: How is Your Credit Score Calculated?

Each credit reporting agency has its own formulas for calculating credit scores. The elements that they use include the type, number, and age of your credit accounts and past applications; the total dollar amount of debt you have and the total dollar amount of available credit you have that you actually use; the number and severity of late payments you have had; and other information found in the public records.

When it comes to fresh start strategies for improving your credit score, the lowest-lying fruit can often be found on your credit report itself. What you're looking for when you review your credit report are factors that could be negatively affecting your score, errors in the report, and inaccurately listed amounts owed for any of your open accounts. For example, because the dollar amount of available credit you have that you use (called your utilization rate) is factored into your credit score, your credit score might be artificially depressed if your lender is showing a lower credit limit on a credit card or home loan line of credit than you were actually approved for. Some of these errors are worth taking the time to fight and have corrected; others are not.

The errors worth the effort to correct include:

- Late payments

- Charge-offs, collections, or other negative items that aren't yours

- Late payments that you actually paid on time

- Debts that you paid off but that are still being shown as outstanding

- Credit limits reported as lower than they actually are

- Accounts listed as "settled," "paid derogatory," "paid charge-off," or anything other than "current" or "paid as agreed," if you paid on time and in full

- Accounts that are still listed as unpaid that were included in a bankruptcy

- Negative items older than seven years (or ten years, in the case of bankruptcy) that should have automatically fallen off your reports

You have to be a bit careful with this last one, because sometimes credit scores can actually go down when negative items fall off your reports. (It's a quirk in the FICO credit scoring software, making the potential effect of eliminating old negative items sometimes difficult to predict.)

Some of the errors you don't need to worry about include various misspellings of your name; outdated or incorrect address information; an old employer listed as current; accounts that you closed incorrectly listed as being open; and accounts that you closed but that don't say "closed by consumer."

One-Minute Mentor: How Long Do Bad Marks Stay on Your Credit Report?

The length of time that it will take for you to rebuild your credit history after a negative change depends on the reasons behind your credit dings. In the new economy, most negative changes in credit scores are due to the addition of specific negatives, such as a loan delinquency or collection account. These new negatives will generally continue affecting your credit scores until they reach a certain age, as follows:

- Delinquency Dings: up to 7 years

- Bankruptcy Dings: up to 10 years

- Unpaid Tax Lien Dings: up to 15 years

- Inquiry Dings: up to 2 years

- Public Record Dings: up to 7 years

Fresh Start Tips for Guarding Your Credit Score

Here are some additional fresh start tips to help you make sure that the new credit score and reporting rules and reforms work for, not against, you.

Send a Letter

If you find errors on your credit report, dispute them with the credit bureau and the reporting agency. You will generally need to write letters to each creditor explaining each error and asking that each error be corrected. Depending on the error and circumstances, you may sometimes need to provide explanations.

Ask for a "Goodwill Adjustment"

If you've been a good customer, a creditor might agree to simply erase that one late payment from your credit history. Your chances of getting a "goodwill adjustment" improve the better your record with the company (and the better your credit in general). But it can't hurt to ask!

Ask to "Re-Age" Your Account

You may also want to ask if your credit can be "re-aged." In that case, the creditor may agree to erase previous delinquencies if you make a series of on-time payments. You can still continue protesting that a charge was unjust, or you can try disputing the account as "not mine" with the credit bureaus.

Take Advantage of Other "Opportunities"

The older and smaller a collection account, the more likely that a creditor won't even bother to verify it when a credit bureau investigates your dispute. A creditor that has merged with another company often leaves its records a real mess, which is a great opportunity you don't want to miss, as it increases your chances that the creditor will be willing to fix something you claim is an error.

Consider "Rapid Rescoring"

Another tip for quicker results is rapid rescoring, but you'll need a creditor who is a customer of a rapid rescoring service. With rapid rescoring, new information that might otherwise take at least thirty days to post can instead be posted in only a few short days. Rapid rescoring is especially valuable when you are trying to improve your credit report before applying for a mortgage loan closing, for example. This service costs about $50 for every account on your credit report that needs to be addressed, but can save you thousands of dollars in interest.

For even more credit score tips see the video clip at www.askshario.com/creditscores.

Life After Foreclosures or Foreclosure Alternatives

If your fresh start includes bouncing back from a foreclosure, short sale, or deed in lieu of foreclosure, not to worry: The new rules and reforms are more forgiving of these types of credit hits than ever before. A lot depends on what your credit score looked like before this home mortgage loan–related event and how much damage was done before the situation was resolved. (In other words, if you were nine payments late before you arranged to do a short sale, that may reflect more poorly in your credit score than if you arranged to do a short sale without ever being late on your mortgage payment.) Nevertheless, here is some guidance (by type of settlement) for your credit score fresh start.

Foreclosure

A foreclosure will bring your FICO score down by as many as 300 points, depending on how bad your credit score looked before the foreclosure, and will stay on your credit report for up to ten years. It may be as long as five years before you can get a decent interest rate on a new home loan and buy a home again.

Deed in Lieu of Foreclosure

A deed in lieu of foreclosure will bring your FICO score down 200 to 300 points. The worse off your credit score was before the deed in lieu, the bigger the hit to your credit score. This mark will stay on your credit report for up to seven years, but you may be able to qualify for a new home mortgage loan in as little as two to three years.

Short Sale

Assuming you're over sixty days late on your mortgage loan payment, doing a short sale, instead of simply allowing your home to be foreclosed, may enable you to get a decent interest rate on a new home mortgage loan again in as little as two years.

The Truth About Credit Repair Companies

Just as the debt collection business has grown by leveraging new opportunities since the Great Recession (discussed later in this chapter), the credit repair industry is also rapidly growing in the new economy. If you are struggling with bad credit, thanks to today's technology, these folks may already know who you are and you may very well already be receiving solicitations from them that make all sorts of promises about fixing your damaged credit score. The truth is that *nobody* can legally remove accurate negative information from your credit report. Credit reporting agencies are obligated under the Fair Credit Reporting Act to correct or delete inaccurate, incomplete, or unverifiable information, usually within thirty days, no matter who asks them to do so. But they are not legally required to remove accurate information unless it is more than seven years old or bankruptcies that are over ten years old.

If you do find errors on your credit report, you have the absolute right to dispute any inaccurate or incomplete information, and the credit reporting agency must investigate the dispute without you incurring a charge. So the value that companies claiming to be able to "repair" your credit really deliver is not that they know some kind of magical secrets, but simply that they do this legwork for you. Rest assured, you are now sufficiently informed to fresh start your own debt and credit score for yourself, but should you want to hire a credit repair professional to handle it for you instead, you'll find plenty of fresh start tips for finding the right credit repair professional in Chapter 7.

Always Go for a Higher Score

Even if your credit happens to be okay, making it even better can pay off big-time. Better credit means that you will pay a lower interest rate (which translates to paying less in interest and less money out of your pocket) and a lower rate for things like insurance. Better credit means you are more likely to get approved for the things you want—for example, a rental apartment. If your fresh start includes buying a home or a car, the interest rate you'll pay for the money you borrow to buy those items will be determined almost entirely by your credit score. Lenders have carved-in-stone rules about handing out the best loan terms and best interest rates to borrowers with a credit score of 700 or better. Most lenders today practice something called "tiered pricing," where the interest rate you pay goes up as your credit score goes down. Lenders choose their own "break points" between each tier, so when you're shopping for your fresh start loans, be sure to look for a lender that offers the best interest rate based on your specific credit score. Even if your credit score is "close"—for example, 698 instead of 700—those two points could cost you thousands of dollars over the life of the loan. For example, on a $165,000 thirty-year, fixed rate home mortgage loan, a mere third of a point could cost you more than $11,172 in interest charges!

Managing Debt in the New Economy

The truth about debt management (which for purposes of simplicity also refers to interest rate arbitration, debt consolidation, and debt settlement) is that it only works if you're on board with making some other changes, too. For most folks, that includes a commitment to swiping those credit and debit cards a whole lot less. You probably already know that. What's different is that it is even more important than it ever was before. No matter how many people you know who carry debt or how you may choose to justify doing so yourself, if you're carrying a heavy load of debt, it will absolutely drag you down and keep moving back the goalposts in your fresh start plan for financial prosperity. No ifs, ands, or buts. What's more, outstanding debt that carries an adjustable interest rate is going to get a whole lot more expensive for you to manage. Now more than ever before, it serves you well to incorporate a plan into your fresh start to get rid of as much debt as you can and convert what you can't get rid of to the lowest possible fixed interest rate repayment plan, before interest rates go up.

Why You Buy

If you can't begin paying down your debt today, at least work on strategies to stop adding more debt. The reason you spend money and buy things may be a helpful topic for you to explore. If you've already trimmed your expenses to the bone and are sure that your inability to avoid further debt is due to an ongoing lack of sufficient income, or if you slipped behind because of a temporary setback, such as in employment or health, then some of the proven strategies in Chapter 6 for spending even less will help you craft a debt-free fresh start. But if the reasons behind your debt and spending are beyond sheer necessity, unraveling the sometimes deeper-rooted psychological reasons why you overspend can permanently change your life for the better. The reasons some folks spend money—including the emotional needs that spending can appear to fulfill; the things that spending buys; and the euphoric highs, sometimes followed by guilt-ridden lows, that spending can elicit (including from actual chemical reactions inside your brain)—exceed the scope of this book. But if the psychological drivers just mentioned hit a chord for you, then the tips in Chapter 7 can help you to find the right professional to help you figure that out.

Identifying the reasons behind your spending is the first step toward developing a plan for chipping away at your debt with the comfort of knowing that you won't "go there" again. The self-assessment in the sidebar will help get your spending and debt fresh start started.

Once you've committed to resolving the reasons for your debt, it's time to begin whittling down the debt itself. Perhaps the most important part of any fresh start plan, even in today's economy, is to establish a realistic plan, which includes clear time frames, and hold yourself to it.

Self-Assessment: Identifying the Reason for Your Debt

	YES	NO
Are you in debt because you have not been able to earn enough money?	☐	☐
Are you in debt because of a temporary financial setback (perhaps medical, family, or job)?	☐	☐
Are you in debt because you spend money when you don't really have to?	☐	☐

If you answered Yes to either of the first two questions, Chapter 6 will provide you with some great fresh start tips for spending less and earning more. If you answered Yes to the third question, then digging deeper to uncover the true reasons for your spending may be essential to your fresh start plan.

The Business of Debt Management

As is the case with credit repair, you may be perfectly capable of whittling down the debt for yourself, but if you feel that some professional guidance would benefit you, there are plenty of resources to turn to for help. The good news is that millions of dollars in new government stimulus money have been earmarked for credit and debt counseling, and the new rules and reforms include several requirements for nonprofit organizations to provide such services, often for free. Since the bailout, the debt management business has soared, as folks across America desperately try to get out from underneath unbearable financial burdens. While there are plenty of honorable debt management companies out there, as you can imagine, not everyone operating in these businesses does so honestly, so the incidence of debt rescue fraud and scammers has risen as well. Fortunately, you will find in Chapter 7 an explanation of how you can get the professional help you may need in this area without getting taken.

Among its many responsibilities, the new Consumer Financial Protection Bureau (CFPB) also has authority over counseling agencies, including debt management plan providers and debt settlement service providers. Of particular importance for counseling agencies and other providers of debt relief services is the fact that the CFPB now—in addition—has the authority to enforce rules issued by the Federal Trade Commission with respect to unfair or deceptive acts or practices, as quickly covered for you in these next sections.

How to Protect Yourself from Aggressive Collection Firms

If you are ready to roll out your fresh start plan but have unpaid debt that's been lingering around for a while, you may wind up face-to-face with collection firms.

In the new economy, debt collection is a multibillion-dollar industry. For decades, debt in America has been increasing (see Figure 3-1), and as of 2011, almost 30 million individuals, or 14 percent of all American adults, had debt that was subject to the collections process. It may come as no surprise to you that debt collectors have more complaints filed against them than any other type of company. The Federal Trade Commission, the agency that was in charge of regulating collection firms until the new rules and reforms took effect, described the debt collection industry as

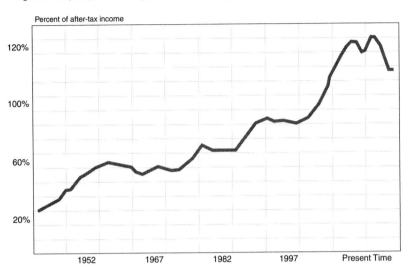

Figure 3-1. Up to (and including) the bubble, average American debt increased significantly.

a "major" consumer protection problem. Complaints about both third-party debt collectors (in other words, companies hired by your original creditor to collect your debt) and in-house collectors (folks who are employees of your actual creditor) totaled almost 150,000 in 2011 and accounted for almost 30 percent of all complaints the FTC received. The most common complaints involve debt collectors repeatedly calling people (which alone accounts for nearly half of all complaints), misrepresenting debt amounts or status, and failing to notify folks of their legal rights in writing. Unlawful threats of arrest or property seizure and using profanity and abusive language are also not uncommon. More than 4,200 people even reported being threatened with violence by a debt collector! More and more folks are having wages garnished without the proper court order, funds withdrawn from their accounts based on unauthorized charges, and even credit cards used without their permission. All of this screaming, name-calling, cursing, and use of false threats is being done not only by rogue individual collectors, but by debt collectors following their full-fledged company policy. In the new economy, even the debt collectors themselves have to work harder than ever before just to get paid, increasing the chances that some of them will cross the line.

The primary federal law protecting you against overly aggressive debt collectors is the Fair Debt Collection Practices Act. Each state also has its own similar law.

What Is the Fair Debt Collection Practices Act?

Congress passed the Fair Debt Collection Practices Act in 1977 in order to eliminate abusive collection practices by debt collectors (and also ensure that those debt collectors who do refrain from using abusive practices are not competitively disadvantaged). The prohibition of deceptive, unfair, and abusive practices applies to third-party debt collectors. For the most part, creditors collecting their own debts are exempt from the Fair Debt Collection Practices Act. The act sets boundaries for debt collection activities, including the time and place collection calls can be made; it restricts how and to whom information about your debt is communicated; and it prohibits deceptive, threatening, and abusive collection tactics. Practices off-limits for debt collectors include harassment and false statements.

Harassment

Debt collectors can't harass or abuse you or any other third party they contact. Harassment includes threats of violence or harm, use of obscene or profane language, and repeat or constant telephone calls.

False Statements

Debt collectors can't lie when they are trying to collect a debt. They cannot falsely claim that they are attorneys or government representatives, falsely claim that you've committed a crime, falsely represent that they operate or work for a credit reporting company, misrepresent the amount of money that you owe, and indicate that papers they send to you are legal forms if they aren't or that papers they send to you aren't legal forms if they are. Debt collectors also are prohibited from claiming that you will be arrested if you don't pay them; that they will seize, garnish, or sell your property or wages (unless they are permitted by law to take that action and actually intend to do so); and that legal action will be taken against you (if doing so would be illegal or if they don't actually intend to take such action). They are further prohibited from trying to collect any interest, fee, or other charge on top of the amount that you actually owe (unless the contract that created your debt or state law allows them to collect that additional amount).

Debt collectors may get out of hand, but at the same time, debt collection is critical to a well-functioning consumer credit market. By collecting delinquent debt, collectors reduce creditors' losses from nonrepayment, thereby helping to keep consumer credit available and presumably more affordable to everyone.

The new rules and reforms recognize that today's debt collection industry is an entirely different animal from the industry contemplated when the Fair Debt Collection Practices Act was written over three decades ago. In days long gone by now, collection activities depended on typewritten notices and telephone calls. Modern-day debt collection firms use much more sophisticated analytics to identify specific debtors and then target calls. Autodialers and Internet telephony have lowered the cost of contacting debtors so that now even small collections firms find it economically feasible to cost-effectively and efficiently reach hundreds of thousands of debtors. Important new economic players (namely, debt buyers and larger collections law firms) have entered the industry, and database improvements have facilitated the sale of debt, creating an entirely new industry of debt buyers.

Today, the Consumer Financial Protection Bureau has authority to oversee the Fair Debt Collection Practices Act and prescribe rules with respect to debt collection, to issue guidance concerning debt collectors' compliance with the law, to collect complaint data, to educate consumers and collectors, and to undertake research and policy initiatives related to consumer debt collection. Certain specific developments under the new debt collection rules and reforms are recapped for you in the next sidebar.

Among the new reforms, the CFPB launched a "Consumer Response" initiative (including a toll-free number and a complaint form on the CFPB website for folks like you to use) to address complaints and inquiries about debt collectors.

Fresh Start Tips for Dealing with Debt Collection

So what can you do if a debt collection agency starts making your life miserable? Here are some debt collection fresh start tips you'll want to know about.

Talk Once

Some experts will tell you to not answer the telephone when a debt collector calls. But if you think that it may not be your debt that they're calling you about, or if you would pay down the debt if you could afford to do so, you may want to talk to the debt collector at

New Rules and Reforms and Collection Agencies

Under the Dodd-Frank Act, the Consumer Financial Protection Bureau now has the authority to supervise many creditors who collect their own debts or hire third-party debt collectors and, depending on how the CFPB's proposed "larger participant" rule plays out, perhaps even larger nonbank debt collectors, too. Specific powers are granted in the Dodd-Frank Act, including the following examples:

Dodd-Frank Section 1022(c)(1) instructs the Consumer Financial Protection Bureau to monitor debt collectors offering or providing services for risks to consumers. To conduct this monitoring, the CFPB is authorized to gather information regarding debt collectors' business and activities, and debt collectors themselves are required to file reports and information the CFPB deems necessary.

Dodd-Frank Section 1025 authorizes the Consumer Financial Protection Bureau to supervise large insured depository institutions and credit unions (with more than $10 billion in assets) and their affiliates, as well as their service providers (which could include third-party debt collectors).

Dodd-Frank Section 1026 additionally allows the CFPB to require reports from smaller insured depository institutions and bureau examiners to determine Fair Debt Collection Practices Act compliance. Section 1026(e) also gives the CFPB supervisory authority over some service providers to smaller depository institutions.

least once. After all, you need to let him know if you're contesting the debt he's trying to collect from you or if you might be able to work out a payment plan with him. In the new economy, debt collectors are often willing to work out payment plans for as little as $5 to $10 a month, in large part because they know the average recovery on debt collections in the new economy can be as little as 20 percent if they don't work with people. If you are going to pay down debt, always be sure to get in writing any agreement with a debt collector. If you do legitimately owe money and want to make a deal to pay it off, *never* give a debt collector your checking account number. Unfortunately, it is common for debt collectors to try to take more money out of an account than they tell you they will take. If you plan to record your telephone calls with a debt collector and state law requires disclosure, be sure to let him know at the beginning of the telephone call.

Taking at least one telephone call with a debt collector also allows you to try to get some information from the collector. For example, if you can get any information about the financial arrangement under which a debt collector is working (in other words, for whom he works and how he is getting paid) that information may give you better leverage to negotiate a payment deal. Debt collectors sometimes work on a shared contingency basis, meaning that the debt collector gets paid a percentage of what he collects from you. Other times, debt collectors buy the debt itself from your original creditor, typically at a big discount, meaning the debt collector has literally *invested* in you and will want to be sure he gets his money back, plus a healthy profit.

Get a Validation Notice

Remember, debt collectors must send you a validation notice within five days of their first contact with you, showing how much money you owe, the original creditor's name, and how you can proceed if you don't think that you owe the money.

Send a Verification Letter

If you send a debt collector a letter saying that you don't owe some or all of the debt or asking for further verification within thirty days of the validation notice, the debt collector has to stop calling you until he provides that further information to you.

Be Ready to Send a No Call Letter

If you don't want to speak with a debt collector again after that, simply tell him so in writing. That letter should be sent by certified mail, return receipt requested. Be sure to keep a copy of this letter, and all of your communications with a debt collector, in a safe place. Upon receipt of such a letter, a debt collector can't legally call you again, but that doesn't mean that the debt goes away. In fact, at that point a debt collector can, and very well may, sue you in court in order to collect the debt.

Prepare for Lawsuits and Complaints

If a debt collector sues you, it is wise to respond to all legal court notices that you receive within the time period allowed (which will be written in the notice itself) and to consult with a lawyer if possible. (Chapter 7 provides some proven tips to help you find the right lawyer.) If a debt collector wins a lawsuit against you, the court will enter a judgment against you and the debt collector can then try to garnish your wages or levy your accounts or other assets in order to collect the money you owe. Generally, federal benefits such as Social Security can't be garnished by a debt collector (although, under some circumstances, such as for taxes, alimony, child support, or student loans, they sometimes can be). You have the right to sue a debt collector or report unfair practices to your state attorney general, the Federal Trade Commission, and the Consumer Financial Protection Bureau if you wish to do so.

Beware the Scams

One increasingly common scam involves corrupt debt collectors illegally trying to collect old, "time-barred" debts. Each state has its own laws, called a statute of limitations, regarding how long a debt can be collected. In Florida, for example, the statute of limitations is three to ten years, depending upon the type of debt. In another well-known scam, fraudsters collected $9.4 million from people who did not even owe any money, but who apparently agreed to pay the fraudulent debt collectors just to get them to stop calling.

Thanks to the Great Recession, more folks than usual have been forced to use credit to make ends meet. In fact, there are presumably plenty of folks living off of credit at this very moment—incurring debt that they may not ever be able to repay. This situation translates to even more and more business opportunity for debt collectors. In 2011 alone, $150 billion in unpaid debt was placed into collection and $40 billion was actually collected! There are 4,100 debt collection agencies in America. The industry is expected to grow by 26 percent over the next three years. If you find yourself coming head-to-head with a debt collector, check out the video clip at www.askshario. com/debtcollectors and be prepared!

Fresh Start After Bankruptcy

Hopefully you will not need to incorporate bankruptcy protection into your fresh start plan. But, because it is such an important option for folks who really do need it, and because national bankruptcy filing rates are a helpful indicator of the health of America's economy for everyone else, a brief discussion about the fresh start role that bankruptcy can play is worthwhile.

Before the Great Recession, the last turning point in the world of bankruptcy was the 2005 Bankruptcy Abuse Prevention and Consumer Protection Act. Interestingly, some experts theorize that one of the reasons bankruptcy filings have not surged since the bailout is because the 2005 law increased the legal and administrative fees necessary to file bankruptcy by about 60 percent and mandated that folks pay for credit counseling before filing. Between 1996 and 2004, more than a million Americans filed bankruptcy each year, and more than 2 million filed in 2005 (and that was during good economic times!). The number of bankruptcy filings dropped to half that number in 2006, once the Bankruptcy Abuse Prevention and Consumer Protection Act took effect. After the real estate bubble burst, bankruptcy filings rose to over one million again and have hovered between 1.3 million and 1.5 million each year since. As you might expect, the number of new economy bankruptcy filings varies by geographic region, with higher concentrations in the harder hit states. For example, California and Nevada have some of the highest bankruptcy filing rates in America. One in every eighty-eight Nevada residents filed for bankruptcy protection in 2011.

Two types of bankruptcy protection are relevant in the new economy for average folks: Chapter 7, in which the debts that you can't pay (after liquidating your assets) are forgiven, and Chapter 13, in which a payment plan is negotiated to pay off your debts. (See the sidebar for more details on the differences.)

Whether you file for bankruptcy under Chapter 7 or Chapter 13, you can expect an automatic "stay" to take effect. This "time-out"

> ### One-Minute Mentor: What's the Difference Between Chapter 7 and Chapter 13 Bankruptcy?
>
> In a Chapter 7 bankruptcy, your nonexempt assets are *liquidated* at the direction of a bankruptcy court in order to satisfy your creditors' claims. Remaining creditors' claims are then discharged, and you are no longer personally liable for those debts. The Bankruptcy Abuse Prevention and Consumer Protection Act of 2005 requires that the bankruptcy court determine whether you qualify for relief under Chapter 7. In other words, if your income is too high, you may not be eligible for Chapter 7 bankruptcy. You can only file for Chapter 7 bankruptcy once every eight years.
>
> A Chapter 13 bankruptcy focuses on *reorganization* and may be more suitable if you have reliable income and simply need some fresh start time to catch up and get your finances in order. Under Chapter 13, you need to make regular payments according to a bankruptcy plan approved by the court. Your disposable income is given to a trustee, who keeps a percentage as a fee and parcels out the rest to the creditors in accordance with the plan. As long as you abide by the plan, you are protected from garnishments, lawsuits, and other creditor actions. After your bankruptcy plan is completed, your remaining debts are discharged. Chapter 13 tends to be more common for homeowners in the new economy since it allows you to stop a foreclosure proceeding, pay back delinquent mortgage payments over time, and keep your home. You're only prevented from refiling for Chapter 13 for six months.

temporarily prevents your creditors from moving forward with debt collection, wage garnishment, and lawsuits related to your finances, foreclosure, or repossessions. Chapter 13 is less damaging to your credit score than Chapter 7. Under Chapter 13, your creditors will see that you are making an effort to pay off your debts. Unfortunately, the reality is that it is sometimes harder to obtain new credit if you file Chapter 13 instead of Chapter 7 because new creditors know that you have to pay off other, already-existing creditors and you will not be able to use your extra cash moving forward to pay them. Each state has certain differing laws regarding bankruptcy, levies, and what funds are or are not protected.

It is worth mentioning that if your fresh start plan involves a bankruptcy, foreclosure, or other traumatic financial event, addressing the emotional side of those situations may be appropriate. You may be so invested in feelings of failure, disappointment, and shock that it becomes extremely difficult to accept these events as merely a *temporary* setback. Let those self-destructive feelings go, and instead commit to learning what you can from the experience and moving forward. The truth is that your actions after a financial crisis can determine how badly and for how long your finances will be negatively affected moving forward.

That is not to say that filing bankruptcy should be endorsed carte blanche. Contrary to the perception some people hold that bankruptcy is for deadbeats, the majority of folks who file for bankruptcy protection do so following entirely unforeseeable circumstances—such as a divorce, health issue, or unavoidable protracted unemployment—and they simply need a second chance to "do the right thing." In fact, filing for bankruptcy as a way to simply avoid having to pay your debts is not as easy as you may think. Folks who try to "max out" their credit cards, file for bankruptcy, and never pay for the things they buy may be surprised to find that bankruptcy judges are wise to this type of fraud. Anyone who thinks that they can simply transfer a home or other assets into a trust or transfer it out of their name altogether and then file for bankruptcy is, likewise, going to find that their creditors are typically able to "unwind" transfers like this by convincing the judge that it was nothing more than an attempt to hinder, delay, or defraud creditors from their lawful rights to collect the debt.

The following self-assessment is designed to help you decide if bankruptcy may be appropriate for you.

Self-Assessment: Should You Consider Bankruptcy?

	YES	NO
Do your unsecured debts equal or exceed your annual income?	☐	☐
Are you struggling to make even minimum payments on your debts?	☐	☐
Are you being sued by a creditor?	☐	☐

If you answered Yes to one or more of the above questions, it may benefit you to at least consider bankruptcy as part of your fresh start strategy.

New Bankruptcy Rules and Reforms

So how do the new rules and reforms impact bankruptcy? In general, bankruptcy for average folks remains the same. Wall Street, banks, and financial institutions, as opposed to individuals like you, are most significantly affected. For example, by extending the Bankruptcy Code to cleared derivative swaps, the new rules and reforms ensure that the various types of financial products dealt with on Wall Street will be treated comparably to each other—essentially creating a significant new regulatory authority but still leaving important concerns unanswered and unintended consequences left to unfold. The new rules and reforms also address the ability of federal regulators to step in if state regulators fail to take action in certain liquidation scenarios.

But for the most part, the new rules and reforms in this area kick in only when insolvency threatens certain companies that could impact the stability of U.S. financial markets. For example, Dodd-Frank provides for a new system of liquidating "systemically important nonbank financial companies" that are in danger of default. Under certain circumstances (spelled out in the new rules and reforms), the Federal Deposit Insurance Corporation (FDIC) is appointed as receiver and proceeds with the "orderly liquidation" of the company, which is similar to bankruptcy.

Affected banks and financial institutions now face different treatment and possibly much different outcomes than before if they or a company they do business with becomes subject to the new "orderly liquidation" authority rather than simply becoming a debtor under the old Bankruptcy Code. These new rules and reforms arguably make it more difficult to manage certain business risks. Because there is some lack of clarity in the intended breadth of the term "financial company," and some discretion afforded to the regulators who will be making these determinations, banks and other financial institutions face uncertainty.

The orderly liquidation authority also removes courts and judges from certain processes and leaves creditors with fewer rights than under the old Bankruptcy Code. As a result, banks and financial institutions are likely to remain wary of the new rules and reforms as compared with the contractual safeguards they have relied on in the past. So what does it mean to you? While the long-term, broad-stroke theme is to curb some of the risky behavior by banks (behavior blamed for causing the bailout), one unintended consequence is that these new rules and reforms may also translate to institutional hesitancy, further dampening the broader economy until banks and financial institutions (and the companies they do business with) are able to get more comfortable with the new rules and reforms.

Fresh Start Tips for Bankruptcy Filings

Even if your situation isn't dire enough to justify bankruptcy, if you are feeling overwhelmed by your debts you might want to consult with a bankruptcy attorney or with an approved credit counselor. That's recommended because you want to ensure that you fully and accurately understand your options and don't overlook any potential opportunities to jump-start your fresh start. Bankruptcy, of course, varies from case to case, but here are some important tips about the more universal issues that you may want to keep in mind.

You Get What You Pay For

If you choose to work with outside professionals, steer clear of petition preparers, typing services, or paralegals who claim they can handle your bankruptcy for a flat fee. If the fee sounds too good to be true ... it probably is.

Track Your Exempt Assets

Bankruptcy laws and exemptions vary from state to state, but every state has exemptions that protect certain kinds of assets, such as your house, your car (up to a certain value), money in qualified retirement accounts, household goods, and clothing.

Accept That Some Debts Can't Be Discharged

Certain types of debts cannot be discharged or erased, including child support and alimony, student loans, restitution for a criminal act, and debts incurred as the result of fraud. Generally speaking, if you file for Chapter 7 or Chapter 13 bankruptcy, you may have certain loans discharged only if the bankruptcy court finds that repayment would impose undue hardship on you and your dependents. This must be decided in an adversary proceeding in bankruptcy court after the conclusion of the bankruptcy. Your creditors will be present to challenge your request. The court uses a three-pronged test to determine hardship: 1) If you are forced to repay the loan, you would not be able to maintain a minimal standard of living; 2) there is evidence that this hardship will continue for a significant portion of the loan repayment period; 3) you made good-faith efforts to repay the loan before filing bankruptcy (usually this means that you have been in repayment for a minimum of five years).

Should Your Spouse File?

If you're married, your spouse does not necessarily have to file for bankruptcy, too. In fact, it's not uncommon for one spouse to have a significant amount of debt in his name only. But if you and your spouse have debts for which you're both liable and that you both want to discharge, you may decide that it is best to file together. Otherwise, your creditors can simply demand payment for the entire amount from the spouse that doesn't file.

Beware of Discharged Debt Reported as Income

Be aware that, at the end of any bankruptcy, you may receive a 1099 form from creditors listing your discharged debt as unreported income. Folks who don't plan for this taxable event may find themselves right back in financial trouble and may not get another chance at a fresh start.

Life After Bankruptcy

The good news is that there is life after bankruptcy. Many folks report that they're able to launch a successful fresh start much quicker by filing bankruptcy and getting started with a solid, predictable fresh start process right away. You may find that it is better than struggling to keep afloat, only to have to grapple with the inevitable at a later date. Why push back the time to begin your fresh start?

In terms of moving forward, filing for bankruptcy is admittedly among the worst negatives you can have on your credit report. But the fear many folks have—namely, that they will never be able to get credit again—is simply not true. In fact, after your bankruptcy case closes, you're likely to receive a barrage of credit card offers. Remember that these credit offers aren't out of the goodness of the credit card companies' hearts. Once you've completed a bankruptcy, you're a safer bet because the credit card companies know that there are several months or years (depending on whether you file under Chapter 7 or 13) before you can file for bankruptcy again and have any new debts discharged! But, of course, the interest rates and risks associated with signing up for new credit cards immediately following a bankruptcy are high. Some experts suggest looking into a secured credit card after your bankruptcy case closes. Most major banks offer secured cards, and borrowers are limited to spending only the money that they put into their account in advance. If your post-bankruptcy fresh start includes a secured card, just be sure the issuer reports to one of the three main credit reporting agencies so that you can use the secured card to improve your credit score moving forward.

Rebuilding your credit is essential to your fresh start post-bankruptcy. While it's always a good idea to stay on top of your credit report, it is absolutely essential to do so after a bankruptcy. Begin by pulling your credit report about two months after your bankruptcy case closes to check for any errors, then follow the tips you found earlier in this chapter to clear up any errors and improve your credit score.

The Bottom Line

It may not be easy, but stabilizing your credit and your debt is time very well spent. It allows you to move forward without the risk of either credit or debt becoming an insurmountable obstacle to your future prosperity. And you will find that, once you've worked hard to get your debt down and your credit score up, you will be far more motivated to keep it that way. In the next chapter, step 3 of your financial fresh start, you'll learn how to protect your savings, investments, and retirement under the new economy, rules, and reforms to ensure your solid future prosperity.

CHAPTER FOUR

Step Three:
Protect Your Savings,
Investments, and Retirement

- **What Will You Learn from This Chapter?** If there's one thing folks learned from the Great Recession it's that you can no longer simply take it for granted that your savings and investments will grow, or that they are even solid places to put your hard-earned money. In less time than it takes you to wash a load of laundry, this chapter guides you through everything you need to know about the new rules and reforms to protect your essential savings and investment assets (the homeownership portion of your assets are covered in the next chapter) and still retire happily ever after.

- **How Will This Know-How Help You?** Ensuring that your savings and investment money is safely at work is essential to guaranteeing financial prosperity and golden years that you can count on!

The Truth About Financial Planning

Whether it's savings accounts, stocks, bonds, real estate, or the endless number of other places you can park your hard-earned cash, investing is a subject that most folks either love or hate—so much so that plenty of people wind up doing virtually nothing about safeguarding and putting their money to work for them. The universal challenge is that, in addition to being able to pay your bills today, no matter how much money you do or don't have (and whether you earn it yourself or it's given to you) *everybody* needs to somehow have access to financial resources to survive if and whenever they don't want to work or are no longer able to do so. (It's also true that setting aside dollars to save and invest is a challenge; this challenge is addressed in Chapter 6.)

Even though this is clearly an area in which everybody's personal situation and predispositions differ, there is one very important common denominator: "Personal Finance" is far more about *personal* than it is about *finance*. No matter what your own situation, your savings, investments, and retirement fresh start hinges on the answers to questions that are uniquely personal to you and that no one other than you—not even the top finance and investment experts—can possibly answer. If you've not yet considered the fundamentals, the self-assessment sidebar provides a helpful starting point for your fresh start.

Of course the world is not perfect. Even the best intentions to save and invest a certain amount of money each year can often be derailed by both expected expenditures (such as college tuition and weddings) and the unexpected (such as job loss, divorce, medical issues, disability, or death). And, as you save and invest, there's no guarantee that your investments will yield the returns you'd hoped. Adding insult to injury, many of these same risks and variables persist into your retirement. Not to mention the fact that God only knows

The "Personal" in Your Personal Finances

How much money do you currently have $_____
in your home, savings, and investments?

In a Perfect World:

How much money are you pretty sure you $_____
can earn and save each year?

How much do you think you can earn off $_____
these savings each year?

How many years do you have until you $_____
plan to retire?

How much money will you have saved by $_____
the time you retire?

How much will it cost you to live each year $_____
when you're retired?

How much do you think you can earn off $_____
your savings once you're retired?

What other sources of income will you have $_____
and how much can you count on from each?

Source: _____ Income $_____

Source: _____ Income $_____

Source: _____ Income $_____

Will your retirement income cover your living expenses? If these numbers don't add up, you may need to earn and save more or work longer until you retire. Return to the first question of the assessment and adjust your answers accordingly.

how long you will live. Perhaps these things that tend to be beyond your control are the reasons why so many folks wind up with no real savings, investment, and retirement plan at all.

One way to get comfortable with this inherent uncertainty and not let it dictate everything, especially in light of the new economy dynamics you're faced with today, is to give yourself permission to simply do the best that you can. Let go of the need for precision. Even for the pros, much financial planning is, in truth, "guesstimating." So make the best educated guesses that you can and then move on. Precisely because of all the uncertainty in the new economy, commit to periodically revisiting your savings, investment, and retirement fresh start plan and adjusting your guesstimates to reflect your life's (and the new economy's) latest actual realities. Getting a fresh start on your financial prosperity is an ongoing process, a lifestyle, not a one time event. Small, simple steps, taken consistently and over time, add up to big life-changing results. Give yourself credit for all the things you do right instead of beating yourself up over the missteps. Don't sweat imperfection; every savings, investment, and retirement plan has some. Certainly some imperfect planning is better than no planning at all!

The other reason many people avoid doing this sort of planning is that it can seem complicated, even overwhelming. This chapter will take care of that fresh start obstacle for you, too.

Losing Trust in Stocks

While your home or other real estate investments are covered for you in the next chapters, the million-dollar fresh start question is: Where else can you safely and productively put your money in the new economy? Notwithstanding surging stock prices and concerns in real estate, many folks in the new economy seem to trust stocks even less than homes as a long-term investment. (See Figure 4-1.) Only 54 percent of Americans now directly own individual stocks. Ongoing challenges in Europe, China, and around the world, such as insider trading and stock market manipulation, only compound the general feeling of apprehension keeping investors on the sidelines. For example, 14 percent of the sales made by companies comprising the S&P 500 come from Europe, and many significant American companies have large European sales. A European recession could easily reduce European consumer demand for American stock and goods.

The right investment choices depend on your particular situation, including how much money you have and how much you owe; your personal needs, wants, and goals; your comfort with risk; and how much time you have until you will need to access your money.

Figure 4-1. Very few Americans invest directly in the stock market.

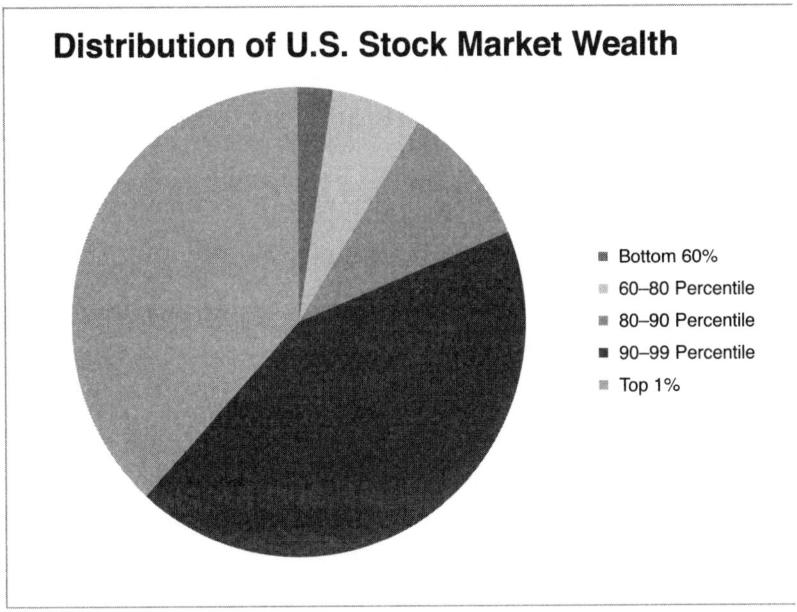

Distribution of U.S. Stock Market Wealth

- Bottom 60%
- 60–80 Percentile
- 80–90 Percentile
- 90–99 Percentile
- Top 1%

Because plenty has already been written about various approaches to saving and investing in general, this discussion will focus more on saving and investing given the dynamics of the new rules, reforms, and economy.

Fortunately, everybody's investing decisions begin with determining their own personal saving and investing IQ. The self-assessment in the sidebar opposite will help you to accomplish this next step.

Getting Inside Your Own Head

If you feel that you may have been avoiding or not handling your savings and investments in the manner you know you should, it is helpful to quickly examine some of the reasons why. Perhaps the most pervasive new dynamic in the new economy is "investing immobility."Since the real estate bubble burst and the world began to feel so turbulent, investing fear is not uncommon. Particularly given the impact of low interest rates (which essentially penalize savers and are presenting a significant challenge to retirees who counted on higher returns) and inflation (discussed in more detail shortly), the pitfalls of this type of paralysis may very well prove to be even more negative for your financial fresh start than the risk of making an occasional wrong investment decision.

Even once you've overcome the fear of making investments, you may find yourself lying awake at night second-guessing your investment decisions.You will find you sleep far more soundly if you simply bear in mind that your investment fresh start strategy is for the long, not short term, and commit (absent any truly significant events in the world or your own life) to reevaluating your investment decisions once a quarter or even once a year.

Self-Assessment: Your Saving and Investing Fresh Start IQ

The answers to this self assessment lay the groundwork for a more effective saving and investment plan.

	YES	NO
Do you know where the money you have already saved and invested is?	☐	☐
Do you know what it means for your savings and investments to be diversified?	☐	☐
Do you know if your own current savings and investments are diversified?	☐	☐
Do you know how the new rules and reforms may affect your savings and investments?	☐	☐
Do you know how rising interest rates may affect your savings and investments?	☐	☐
Do you know how inflation may affect your savings and investments?	☐	☐
Do you know how the value of the U.S. dollar may affect your savings and investments?	☐	☐
Do you know how the other new economy factors, including America's debt ceiling, trade deficits, developments in Europe, and the global economy, may affect your savings and investments?	☐	☐
Do you know what the five common investment categories for Americans are and how much of your own money is invested in each?	☐	☐

If you answered No to any of the above questions, this chapter will help raise your financial IQ.

Five Basic Savings and Investments Meet the New Economy, Rules, and Reforms

Perhaps the most fundamental way to actually overcome a fear of investing is to improve your investment IQ. Don't worry about knowing everything. In fact, trying to do that freaks out some folks even more. If you need some guidance, tips for finding a professional are covered in Chapter 7. Instead, as you kick off your financial fresh start, focus on the impact the new economy, rules, and reforms may have on five of the more common places you can put your money: bank and credit union accounts, CDs, bonds, mutual funds, and stocks. In addition, bear in mind the three key trade-offs, which inevitably need to be balanced, when you do put money in any of these investments: 1) the interest or return you earn on your investments; 2) the term or duration of your investments and liquidity; and 3) the risks that your investment will not earn the anticipated return or that some or all of your principal may even be lost.

The five common savings and investment alternatives that most folks still choose when crafting a saving and investing fresh start in the new economy are quickly summarized for you in the following sections.

1. *Bank and Credit Union Accounts.* High yield bank accounts, including savings accounts, reward checking accounts, and money market bank accounts, can generate a higher return for you than normal savings accounts and are completely liquid. Although the returns are still among the lowest of any place you can put your money (other than underneath your mattress), the trade-off is liquidity and safety. Under the new rules and reforms, the Federal Deposit Insurance Corporation (FDIC) now guarantees up to $250,000 (an increase from

$100,000, although this amount may change again at a future date) in any FDIC-insured bank in the country, so you can rest assured that your hard-earned money is safe and sound. Amounts over $250,000 per account can be covered by meeting the separate bank or separate "ownership category" requirements. Bank money market accounts are also FDIC insured and liquid (typically with some restrictions that most folks can easily live with). Interest is generally higher than that paid on bank or credit union accounts.

Credit union accounts are insured by the National Credit Union Share Insurance Fund, a government-backed insurance fund for credit union deposits similar to FDIC insurance for banks. For more information, check the video clip at www.askshario.com/moneysafe.

2. *Certificates of Deposit.* Another safe money place in the new economy, also protected up to $250,000 under the new rules and reforms by the FDIC, is a bank certificate of deposit (CD). Certificate of deposit terms generally range from three months to five years, with higher interest being paid in exchange for your longer-term commitment (and penalties imposed for early withdrawal). CDs tend to pay higher interest than bank or credit union and money market accounts.

3. *Bonds.* Certain bonds have become increasingly popular new economy investments as folks favor safety over return on investment. Buying bonds is essentially a way for you to lend your money to different businesses, governments, and other entities. Your loan is paid back, after the agreed amount of time, with an agreed amount of interest (unless you decide

not to hold the bond until it matures, in which case you are penalized by being repaid a lesser amount). Corporate bonds, like the corporate borrowers behind them, experienced turbulence in the wake of the financial crisis, but highly rated corporate bonds have since regained investor favor as the interest rates paid tend to be higher than the interest rates paid for some other bond types (in exchange, of course, for the added risks).

Municipal bonds also tend to be considered relatively low risk and offer other tax advantages, but they have garnered investor skepticism as some of the municipal borrowers behind them experience budget crises. U.S. Treasury bonds have long been considered to be the safest alternative simply because they are backed by America's federal government and guaranteed not to go into default (notwithstanding the near default on America's debt in the fall of 2011, discussed in Chapter 1). Of course, this low risk comes at the cost of earning a lower interest rate, but tax benefits oftentimes level that playing field. The fact that some of these bonds are "tax-free" can help improve your profit on an otherwise lower-paying investment—a subject addressed in the sidebar on Factoring in Taxes.

4. *Mutual Funds.* A mutual fund is nothing more than a collection of stocks, bonds, or possibly other investments purchased with money pooled from many investors, normally based on a predetermined strategy (which may include simply mimicking an index, such as the NASDAQ or the S&P 500, or buying companies of a certain size or within a certain sector, for example). Mutual funds offer you the benefit of being able to diversify your investments (a subject discussed

in more detail shortly) without having to invest the time and effort yourself. In theory, this type of investment protects you against isolated volatility associated with investing in a single company. The bad news is that you pay a fee for this service that may or may not make sense, depending on how much more you can earn by investing this way. Since mutual fund fees vary widely, comparing and understanding them is a good idea.

5. *Stock.* Purchasing a share of stock is essentially buying a piece of the ownership in the public companies in which you choose to invest. As such, the amount of money that you earn or lose on your investment in stock will depend on the success of the companies you invest in (or, more particularly, since a company's stock price depends, in part, on how many other investors want to own it, how popular the company's stock is among investors). In addition to the value of the stock itself, some companies pay dividends, essentially paying you part of the company's profit, in the form of cash or more stock shares. In return for the higher risks associated with investing in stock in comparison to the other types of investments we've just discussed, you can potentially earn (or lose) more money.

Preparing Your Fresh Start for Rising Interest Rates

Many individuals and institutions that borrow money have enjoyed a prolonged period of low interest rates at the same time that folks who save and invest have struggled with corresponding low interest rate returns on their investments. As America's economy improves, it seems inevitable that interest rates will increase.

Factoring in Taxes

The interest that you earn on investments, in general, is taxable. Some of the five common investments offer more favorable tax treatment than others, a factor worth considering in your savings and investing fresh start, particularly if you are fortunate enough to be in a higher tax bracket. Additionally, you know that The America Company needs to pay down its debt and balance its budget (see Chapter 1). Doing so will require more income, which means taxes. As Washington gets back to business following the election, it will behoove you to keep an eye on new tax initiatives and how they might impact your savings and investing.

It is, therefore, helpful for you to consider how rising interest rates could affect your savings and investing fresh start.

Higher interest rates on bank, credit union, and money market accounts and certificates of deposit will be wonderful news, particularly to folks nearing retirement who tend to be more heavily invested in these more conservative places. And there is virtually no downside for you, other than the fact that borrowers to whom the banks generally turn around and lend out this money will wind up paying a *higher* rate of interest to borrow that money as well.

It goes without saying that if the rate of return you can earn on a CD that you choose to buy after interest rates increase will be more than the rate of return you can earn on a CD now, for example, you may want to avoid locking up your money for a long time at today's current lower rates; this is one reason so much investment money is sitting on the proverbial sidelines. Likewise, for example, as interest rates rise, the prices of previously issued bonds tend to decrease. If you buy bonds while interest rates are low and your bonds earn those low rates, who is going to want those bonds when interest rates rise and newer bonds earn higher rates?

Rising interest rates affect companies and industries, and therefore their stock values, differently. For example, higher interest rates increase costs (and thus decrease profits) for growth-minded companies needing to borrow money to expand, meaning that their stock values may fall. Rising interest rates can have a positive or negative impact on the stock market, but generally speaking, rising interest rates initially tend to discourage other investors from investing

One-Minute Mentor: What Makes Interest Rates Go Up or Down?

Interest rates are constantly changing in response to a number of factors, including changes in the supply and demand of credit, Federal Reserve policy, fiscal policy, exchange rates, economic conditions, market psychology, and changes in expectations about inflation. Interest rates have been artificially low for some time because the Federal Reserve has been buying its own long-term U.S. Treasury securities in order to force down interest rates and encourage borrowing and spending. It's one short-term triage initiative to revive the economy, growth, employment, and The America Company's GDP, and investors seeking a safe place for their money have poured into U.S. Treasury securities. The Fed uses artificially low interest rates as a way to increase the supply of money in circulation. It's a simple premise that interest rates help control the flow of money in our economy. But it's also a careful balancing act, since too much money in circulation can cause inflation. As the economy recovers, the Fed will presumably ease the rates of interest upward, in order to decrease the supply of money in circulation and manage inflation.

in stocks and accordingly initiate an (albeit temporary) period of lower returns on your own stock investments.

Inflation and Your Savings and Investments Fresh Start

In comparison to the double-digit inflation of the early 1980s, inflation rates have dropped significantly. But some experts believe that higher inflation is a dynamic that you may face moving forward into the new economy. Sometimes inflation happens overnight, but today's flavor seems to be less obvious. Take, for example, increases in the cost of daily essentials, such as clothing, food, and fuel as reflected in Figure 4-2.

Figure 4-2. Inflation's upward trend is causing the price of essentials to increase, too.

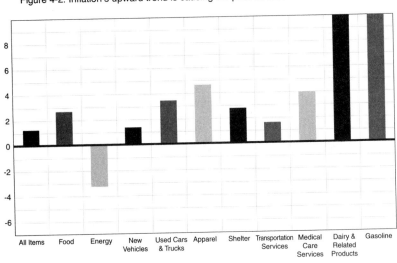

If you're not paying attention, even relatively low inflation, over time, can eventually take its toll on your savings and investments. Inflation, described briefly in Chapter 1, reduces the "real" rate of return you earn on your investments. The reason: While the cost of everything in the world is going up, your money is tied up earning relatively less than those cost increases; when you finally do get your money back, you will not be able to buy as much with it as you were able to buy with it before. So even to just keep you in the same place that you are today financially, your savings and investments need to at least keep pace with inflation. In simplest terms, if the rate of inflation is 3 percent, for example, and you are earning one percent interest in your savings account, you are effectively losing 2 percent of your buying power.

The good news is that there are investments that help you mitigate the effects of inflation and, particularly because inflation is an anticipated dynamic in the new economy, they should be a consideration in your savings and investing fresh start. For example, as you know, your stock investment is an ownership stake in companies. Companies have the ability to raise the prices of their own products and services, which can be an effective inflation-fighting tool. And certain bonds, certificates of deposit, and other products are designed with rates adjusted for inflation, which along with tools such as "diversification" (discussed below), help you manage the impacts of new economy challenges, including rising interest rates and inflation.

Keeping Your Money Safe: Diversifying in the New Economy

Diversification is another way that you can help protect your savings and investments. For example, the stock and bond markets often move in different directions: When the bond market goes up, the stock market often goes down, and vice versa. Diversifying your investments simply means that if you invest in both stocks and bonds, your higher-than-expected earnings from one will compensate for your lower-than-expected earnings in the other. You want diversification both *among* and *within* your investment buckets.

Diversification Among Investments

Though there's some variation among experts, the following rules of thumb may help you determine your diversification fresh start among investment categories:

Do you have a long investment time horizon?

- If yes and you're comfortable with some risk: Allocate 60 percent of your investments to stocks, 30 percent to bonds, and 10 percent to cash equivalents.

- If yes but you're not a risk taker: Allocate 60 percent to bonds, 25 percent stocks, and 15 percent to cash equivalents.

Do you have a short time horizon?

- If yes and you're comfortable with some risk: Allocate 55 percent to bonds, 30 percent to cash equivalents, and 15 percent to stocks.

- If yes but you're not a risk taker: Allocate 55 percent to cash equivalents, 40 percent to bonds, and 5 percent to stocks.

Five years is commonly used as a threshold for investment allocation. If your time horizon is less than five years, your savings and investments need to be more heavily weighted in bonds and cash equivalents. If your time horizon is greater than five years, your savings and investments can have a higher percentage of riskier stocks. Another common rule of thumb is to own a percentage in stocks equal to 115 minus your age.

Diversification Within Investments

Most folks are also able to diversify within one of the five common investment categories fairly easily, too. Take bonds, for example. You can diversify the risks within your bond investment bucket by buying bonds with different characteristics including:

- Bonds from different *issuers* (which helps to protect you from the possibility that an issuer will be unable to meet its obligations to pay you interest or even your principal back).

- Different *types* of bonds (for example, some government, some corporate, and some municipal bonds, which helps to protect you from the possible losses in one of these sectors).

- Bonds with different *maturities* (which helps protect you if interest rates go up; buying bonds or other investments, such as certificates of deposit, with varying maturity dates is sometimes referred to as a "ladder").

Your stock investments, too, can be diversified based on characteristics such as industry or cap rate, for example. Likewise, you can invest in a mix of mutual funds. Some mutual funds focus on growth companies, others are more conservative. Some invest in bonds, others buy only stocks—which leads to a side note worth mentioning: With mutual funds, it makes senses to dig deeper; case in point: Investing in bonds and also investing in mutual funds that invest in bonds is not maximizing diversification.

Expecting the Expected and the Unexpected

Your savings and investing fresh start decisions can prove to be super-helpful to you in structuring and disciplining yourself to expect both the expected and the unexpected expenses in life. For example, if you have a young child and want your savings and investing fresh start to factor in college tuition ten years from now, it may behoove you to periodically invest in fixed rate alternatives, trading higher interest rates for predictability and removing those funds from investments you might otherwise liquidate and spend. A defined maturity date helps you make sure the money is there when you need it.

Putting Your Money Where Your Conscience Is

It goes without saying that the primary objective is earning money from your investments. But you are also supporting the organizations you invest with and in. If you feel strongly for or against certain industries, companies, or causes, here's your opportunity to put your money where your conscience is, assuming it's also a good investment. One such example is described in the next sidebar.

One-Minute Mentor: What Is Microlending?

Want a feel-good, higher-yielding alternative investment? Micro-loans may be for you. These fixed interest loans are made to small business owners in developing countries. Micro-lending sites such as MicroPlace, an eBay subsidiary, match lenders and borrowers across the world. Minimum investments are as small as $20, and you can even choose a specific country, cause, or company to invest in.

Retirement-Specific Fresh Start Savings and Investing

At the end of the day, saving and investing is all about being prepared for life's expensive events, the ultimate of which is often your retirement. In addition to the five common savings and investing alternatives, as covered in the last section, you are no doubt aware of specific vehicles (or ways in which you can *buy and hold* various types of investments, as opposed to actual types of investments themselves) created for retirement savings and investing. They include the 401(k), individual retirement accounts (IRAs), and pension funds. Some of

One-Minute Mentor: Retirement-Specific Fresh Start Saving and Investing Vehicles

Here are some of the more common retirement savings and investment vehicles:

401(k). A 401(k) is a type of retirement savings account with tax benefits, named after subsection 401(k) of the Internal Revenue Code.

INDIVIDUAL RETIREMENT ACCOUNT (IRA). An IRA is a custodial retirement savings account, introduced with the enactment of the Employee Retirement Income Security Act (ERISA) of 1974, that provides tax advantages. Since that time, Roth IRAs, SEP IRAs, and Simple IRAs have also evolved. These types of IRAs vary with regard to the size of company that can establish them, whether they are established by an employer or individual, how they are funded, if and when tax is due, maximum funding caps, vesting, and how and when funds can be withdrawn.

PENSION PLANS. A pension is a set amount of money paid to retired employees by their former employers on a regular basis, usually under a form of legally binding contract. Pension plans can provide for employer contributions, employee contributions, or both during employment.

these vehicles are likewise affected by the new economy, rules, and reforms, as described in the sidebar.

Retirement savings and investing vehicles vary in terms of fees and costs, seasoning periods, contribution limitations, income and earning restrictions, employer contributions, spousal participation, treatment upon death, taxes, conversion rules, exceptions for permitted withdrawal purposes and amounts, permitted and required withdrawal timelines, ages, amounts, penalties, allowable assets, leverage options, and management. Because of the tax-sheltered advantages of some retirement savings and investing vehicles, your fresh start plan might consider using them for your more profitable fresh start investing as opposed to lower-earning investments.

Your 401(k) and the New Rules and Reforms

Over 75 million Americans have a 401(k) with assets collectively totaling more than $3 trillion. And incredibly, many of those folks have no idea what they are paying the investment firms that manage their 401(k) accounts! But, thanks to the new rules and reforms, that will change. Quarterly 401(k) statements are now legally required to reflect the total of all of the fees that you are being charged for your 401(k), clearly and on the very front page. The new 401(k) fee disclosure law is a step toward transparency (which you know is a broad-stroke theme of the new long-term rules and reforms). It is one of the many changes affecting the securities industry.

Investment firms handling 401(k) accounts are also expected to give you a higher "fiduciary" standard of conduct—when advisers treat client investments as they would their own investments—rather than the lower "suitability" standard they provided before the new rules and reforms (see the sidebar for definitions of these standards).

Be aware that firms are not required to adopt the fiduciary standard, but they are required to *disclose* to you whether they are serving you as a fiduciary. This difference can be a game-changer when it comes to the quality of investment advice and investment choices you're provided for your 401(k). Particularly in situations where 401(k) advisers make inappropriate recommendations resulting in legal claims, the difference between a suitability and fiduciary standard can be the difference between winning and losing for you.

One-Minute Mentor: What's the Difference Between "Suitability" and "Fiduciary" Standards?

SUITABILITY STANDARD. Under the suitability standard, a 401(k) investment only has to be "suitable" for you in order for your 401(k) adviser to suggest it. That means, for example, that your 401(k) adviser is legally permitted to encourage you to buy his own company's in-house investments, even if those investments charge you a higher commission and even if alternative similar products are actually also available to you at a lower cost—a clear potential for conflict of interest.

FIDUCIARY STANDARD. Under a fiduciary standard, your 401(k) adviser is legally bound to do what is *best* for you and essentially treat your money as if it's his own. Obviously, the fiduciary standard is a higher standard for 401(k) advisers to meet than the suitability standard, and arguably more beneficial for your savings and investing fresh start. Yet it may surprise you to know that before the new rules and reforms, the majority of employee retirement plans actually operated under the suitability standard.

Your IRA and the New Economy, Rules, and Reforms

IRAs are divided by type: About a third of those folks who have an IRA have traditional IRAs. Another third have rollover IRAs, fewer than a third have Roth IRAs, and only about 10 percent have SEP and Simple IRAs. But here's the shocker: Less than half of all folks who contribute to their IRA (among the lowest-lying fruit, in terms of savings and investing fresh start opportunities) contribute the maximum amount of money allowed! For most people, the reason is fear of committing to set aside that money each year, or just plain inability to do so—a subject covered in more detail, along with issues of earnings and spending, in Chapter 6.

Your Pension Plan and the New Rules and Reforms

Credit default swaps, or "swaps," were touched on briefly in Chapter 1. Pension plans use these swaps to manage interest rate risks and other volatility in connection with your pension plan's own funding obligations to its retirees. In fact, many of the losses caused by the financial contagion of 2008 (described in Chapter 1 as "wide-spreading tree roots") spread to some of the nation's largest pension funds and thus the wallets of millions of Americans. Proposed new rules and reforms would prohibit swap dealers from entering into swaps with pension plans. What's more, under the proposed new rules and reforms, pension plans are also included in the definition of "high-risk financial entities" and therefore subject to the most stringent new rules (which include costly new requirements to post collateral and limit the types of assets that can be used as collateral). The bottom line is that an unintended consequence of the new rules and reforms is that they may help protect pension funds, but they may increase the cost to manage pension plans. Particularly, if pension plans are unable to use swaps, the costs and risks to funding pension plans may increase and potentially affect the retirement savings and investing of millions of folks, perhaps even forcing America's employers to collectively reserve billions of dollars to ensure against this increased funding volatility. How's that for unintended consequences?

How the New Economy Is Hurting Public Pension Plans

The new economy itself is also taking a toll on certain pension funds, which had typically assumed about an 8 percent annual return, but in reality lost almost 20 percent in a single year when the bubble burst. Individual states throughout America, for example, are collectively short by as much as $1.26 trillion in funding their public employee pension accounts and other retirement benefits, a gap that may take years to bridge. Not only have these pension funds been earning lower returns, along with everybody else, but the shortfall comes as a double whammy along with forced cuts in the contributions that many states can afford to make to their pension funds, thanks to other budgetary issues that government is facing. In fact, these pension fund shortages are a primary concern for ratings agencies and investors in the $2.9 trillion municipal bond industry (and a reason some experts suggest that, if your fresh start plan involves investing in municipal bonds, you may want to focus on bonds created to fund essential public projects that a municipality cannot allow to go into default). Because they are legally responsible for paying these benefits, many states may wind up having to cut services they would otherwise be able to provide for folks like you. As a result, some states are lowering benefits for their new workers, essentially kicking the can down the road for America's next generation to deal with the lack of sufficient retirement funds. When pension plan returns are low, states are forced to increase their own contributions. Over the last decade, the added contributions that some states have had to make to cover their pension plan shortages have increased by 152 percent.

Private Pension Plans Also at Risk

Private pension plans, on the other hand, generally assumed a rate of return in the 5.0 to 5.5 percent range—perhaps more realistic but certainly not without risk, given what you know can be prudently expected for savings and investing in the new economy. And lower interest rates are not the only threat to private pensions. The Great Recession taught everybody that even the financial viability of companies that appear to be rock solid should not be taken for granted. It is no longer unheard of for once-sound companies to wind up filing for bankruptcy protection in the new economy. When that happens, private pension funds are, unfortunately, likewise at risk. When a company files for bankruptcy protection, the pension plans its employees counted on are often cut, sometimes significantly. (For example, errors were discovered in the United Airlines employee pension plan after that company filed for protection. At one point these pension plans had only about $8.3 billion in assets to cover almost $18.5 billion in its employee benefit obligations.) Hundreds of thousands of folks who worked in the banking and financial industries pre-bailout lost, collectively, billions of dollars in their company savings and investing stock programs—money they had been counting on having for their retirement. The moral of this story is that if your savings and investing fresh start includes a pension or other company-dependent investment plan, make sure you can count on it in today's new economy or else have a "plan B."

Avoiding Three Common Retirement Planning Pitfalls

You no doubt realize that you are not the only person saving and investing for retirement. And yet most folks tend to not take the time to check out the common mistakes made by those who have come before them, notwithstanding the fact that this is perhaps the simplest way to avoid those same pitfalls yourself. So what are three common financial pitfalls retirees make that you probably want to avoid in your financial fresh start?

Risking Your Retirement Money for Your Kids

If you're like most folks, you care more about your kids than anything else in the world, so you understand how it is that so many folks wind up risking their own financial security to bail out their children (or grandchildren). Those puppy-dog-eyed requests for contributions for home or car down payments or to help with college expenses can seem to be magically timed with your retirement savings and investing horizons. The solution here is super-simple: Unless it is a life-or-death situation, put your own essential financial needs first. Just like they tell you in the airline safety warnings, if the oxygen masks drop, first put on your own mask, that way you will be better able to assist your child with his. Besides that, you will often find that your child or grandchild actually has alternative resources, other than your retirement funds. For example, you can take out loans for college (but you can't take out a loan to pay for your retirement).

Missing Out on Tax Opportunities

As you near retirement, taking the time to project income and tax brackets in order to determine how and when to time certain payments, including payments from retirement accounts, is time well spent. For some folks, retirement account disbursements may increase retirement income, resulting in otherwise avoidable additional taxes, for example. If that describes your situation, a plan of gradual withdrawals starting earlier may make sense.

Another often-missed tax opportunity stems from the regular volunteer work retirees sometimes enjoy. More folks than you might guess leave tax deductions for mileage and out-of-pocket costs associated with their volunteer work on the table. Do you plan to spend the winter down south? If so, changing your legal residency to a state with lower or no income tax, such as Florida (assuming you meet minimum residency and other requirements), can save you thousands of dollars each year *and* may have estate-planning benefits, to boot.

Underestimating the Costs of Healthcare and How Long You Will Live

Old age is now the longest stage in the life of an average American. If your retirement savings and investments are not designed to last thirty years, you may want to revisit that aspect of your fresh start. The next section covers what you can and cannot count on from Social Security and Medicare when you retire. In the new economy, average newly retired American couples need around $250,000 just to pay for medical expenses (excluding long-term care). "Medigap" supplemental insurance, which helps to fill the gaps between what you will need and what Medicare will likely pay for, is one option. If you can afford, it, long-term care insurance, which pays for in-home care and nursing home care, may also be part of your retirement fresh start.

What You Can and Can't Count on from Government Entitlements in the New Economy

You know from Chapter 1 that the viability of America's entitlements, and in particular Social Security and Medicare, are at risk and significantly adding to the country's new economy budgetary challenges. By some estimates, if nothing changes, Social Security and Medicare money will run out sometime between now and thirty years from now.

What does this situation mean to your savings, investing, and retirement fresh start? In spite of the fact that no one seems to be able to agree (or perhaps admit) on the extent of the funding deficits or the timing for entitlement Armageddon, it does seem increasingly obvious that something will have to be done to bring Social Security and Medicare in line with this reality. Fortunately, it's not all bad news for your financial fresh start. The truth is that many Americans have begun living *and working* longer than entitlements, first established decades ago, accounted for. In terms of your own savings, investing, and retirement fresh start, the situation calls for one of my grandfather's "golden rules," namely, to hope for the best, but plan for the worst.

Medicare

With regard to Medicare in particular, the government's healthcare program for the elderly, the fact is that Medicare is not likely to cover your long-term care. In the new economy, long-term extended care costs between 150 percent and 400 percent of the annual income of average America seniors. Of course, if you're almost broke, you may qualify for state-run Medicaid, but the whole point of your savings, investing, and retirement fresh start is to not to *have* to count on that.

As of now, there are just under 50 million folks on Medicare at an annual cost to The America Company of almost a half-trillion dollars. By 2050, America's population counting on Medicare is predicted to be almost 90 million. Under the new rules and reforms, an independent advisory board is scheduled to begin making recommendations on new Medicare rules and reforms around 2015. The bottom line for your savings, investing, and retirement fresh start may again be to assume there'll be fewer government entitlement benefits and to plan for more of these costs to have to come out of your own pocket, one way or another.

Are You Saving—Or Just Talking About It?

During the decade preceding the Great Recession, American households saved less than 4 percent a year. That habit is bound to catch up with folks, and it's one of the reasons why net worth for soon-to-be retirees, ages 55 to 65, has declined and is now hovering at around $250,000 (including whatever home equity is left). If you're like most folks near or in retirement, you may feel as if you have some catching up to do. Almost half don't have a retirement account and less than a quarter even own a single stock or bond. Yet two-thirds believe that it is important to have a specific amount of money saved before retirement. That just doesn't add up.

Reinventing Yourself in Retirement: America's Growing Workforce

Even if folks who have not saved and invested sufficiently can somehow put away more money now, average returns on investments are not expected to increase significantly and many of the new economy risks will persist; thus, making up for lost time, compounded by the recent losses that nobody planned for, may take awhile.

Fortunately, there are other options, including some of the fresh start tools covered in Chapter 6 for earning and saving more before you retire. And there is comfort in knowing that you are not alone. More than half of all soon-to-be retirees need to significantly reduce their current spending in order to save for retirement after years of under-saving, low interest rates on investments, and now not trusting the stock market (when higher returns could otherwise potentially be earned) as a place to invest. Many folks are already planning to work a bit longer before retiring, work full- or part-time after retirement, or both.

Since the bubble burst, the number of working Americans who are age 65 or older has jumped by 16 percent, a trend that actually began almost thirty years ago as wages for American workers, as discussed in Chapter 1, began dropping. During the past decade, full-time work in retirement, as opposed to part-time work, has become increasingly common. (Remember, since 2000, Social Security has not penalized older workers who continue to earn money; work today tends to be less physically taxing than it was in days gone by; and older folks are also healthier.) In fact, thanks to new economy dynamics, 75 percent of soon-to-be retirees plan to work, at least part-time, during their retirement years—39 percent of them because they *have* to, but the rest because they *want* to. Among the reasons cited for wanting to work after retirement are the camaraderie, a desire to remain physically and mentally healthier (retirees who work after retirement tend to be more active and socially connected, which translates to better overall health and fewer medical issues), and the continued need to have a sense of purpose and meaning in daily life. Folks working past retirement age for financial reasons often find that, in addition to increased *income,* there may also be *expense-cutting* benefits, including employee discounts but also employer-based health coverage and lower-cost life insurance—both of which can be costly and challenging to purchase on your own postretirement. Folks remaining in their primary preretirement field of work tend to earn more, but for others, retirement serves as the ideal catalyst to launch a second career or pursue a passion. The only caveat here is that if your retirement fresh start includes plans to work after retirement, regardless of whether your reason is necessity or desire, it is advisable to begin postretirement work sooner rather than later (in other words, don't wait too long to go back to work); going back to work tends to become increasingly difficult the older you get.

Your Money and Your Health

It is not news that stress, including money-induced stress, can lead to both physical and mental health issues, including high blood pressure or depression. In the wake of new economy dynamics such as home mortgage loan foreclosures and plummeting home values and personal net worth, often to the point of negative equity and unemployment, senior Americans in particular are exhibiting elevated rates of depression, which often results in a domino effect of even further unhealthy trade-offs, including lack of sleep or exercise or compromising on necessities like food or medications.

For older homeowners with common chronic conditions (for example, diabetes), health concerns may worsen with financial hardship. As you craft your own personal savings, investing, and retirement fresh start, perhaps bear in mind that the financial security you are creating for yourself may very well translate into a longer, healthier life. In other words, to help make the sacrifices you may need to make today a little bit more palatable, just remember that saving and investing for a more prosperous tomorrow may have positive long-term health consequences.

Borrowing and Retirement

Not unlike any other stage in life, it is not unheard of to need or want to borrow money as you near retirement, or even during your retirement. The difference, however, is that during this particular time of your life, the relatively bigger costs, risks, and stress associated with taking on additional debts can potentially take a bigger toll. And there's a lot less time left to make up for money mistakes later in life.

Of course, everybody's situation differs and there are circumstances in which borrowing is necessary (or just makes sense, even if you have the cash). If your retirement fresh start plan involves the types of borrowing covered in this section, then the few minutes that it will take you to cover this subject will be time well spent.

Borrowing from Your Retirement Savings and Investments

You are allowed to borrow directly from certain retirement savings and investing vehicles or leverage them for borrowing. Internal Revenue Service (IRS) restrictions apply to how and when such loans must be repaid—for example, some loans must be repaid within five years unless the money you borrow is used for the purchase of a primary residence, while other loans require that equal payments be made at least every quarter. These restrictions and other tax considerations merit first consulting with a qualified tax professional. Your employer may, likewise, impose other restrictions on such borrowing. The problem is, if you borrow against your retirement savings and investing plan and then don't or can't make payments in accordance with IRS regulations or your plan's requirements, your unpaid outstanding loan balance can be declared in default and become a taxable distribution to you (together with interest, tax penalties, and all of the other costly implications of unpermitted early withdrawal).

New rules and reforms have been proposed that would allow for the early withdrawal of retirement funds, without paying a penalty to the IRS, in order to cure a home loan mortgage default or otherwise pay for your home. The proposed HOME Act (and legislation like it) would enable you to withdraw up to $50,000 or half of your 401(k) account, whichever is smaller, in order to make your home mortgage loan payments, but your deferred income tax would not be waived. For some folks, this in truth may be like taking from Peter to pay

Paul. Facing a lack of sufficient funds when you need to retire and have fewer alternatives may sometimes be worse than accepting a foreclosure alternative today and moving forward with a clean slate for your fresh start. Only you can decide whether it is worth risking your retirement savings and investments—essentially your financial security for tomorrow—to solve a home mortgage loan or other financial challenge today.

New Rules and Reforms for Reverse Mortgage Loans

Another borrowing vehicle associated with retirement is the FHA Home Equity Conversion Mortgage, commonly referred to as the "reverse mortgage" (although there are also other types of reverse mortgage loans).

Reverse mortgage loans tend to be more complicated than traditional home mortgage loans. For this reason, when it comes to reverse mortgage loans, reading, understanding, and thoroughly thinking through and applying the proverbial fine print is essential, because there are various ways in which your own situation may play out. For example, under some scenarios if an older spouse dies or a younger spouse is not listed as a borrower on the reverse mortgage loan (to maximize the amount of the loan, which is based on age), the younger spouse may be forced to pay off the loan. If a parent dies, children may be forced to pay off the loan. If a borrower moves into an assisted living facility or nursing home, the reverse mortgage loan may need to be paid off. The income stream from a reverse mortgage loan may impact a borrower's ability to qualify for Medicaid.

Reverse mortgage loans are also more expensive than traditional home mortgage loans. The interest rates have historically been 0.25 to 0.50 points higher, and origination and other fees have also always

One-Minute Mentor: What Is a Reverse Mortgage?

A reverse mortgage is a loan secured by your home. No income or credit is required, but you do need to be over the age of 62 at the time that the loan is made. You will not be required to make any repayments until you die, move, or sell your home, at which time that loan has to be repaid to the bank. The concept was invented decades ago in order to help cash- and asset-strapped seniors finance their retirement with the equity they had saved up in their homes (which, for many seniors, at least before the real estate bubble, was their biggest or only asset). If the country's elderly cannot support themselves, then The America Company (i.e., your tax dollars) will have to—making reverse mortgage relevant to everybody.

With a reverse mortgage, rather than *you* making payments to the bank to pay down the loan, the *bank* makes payments to you. Reverse mortgage loans are "nonrecourse," meaning that the bank can't pursue you or your heirs if the sale of your home doesn't generate enough money to repay the reverse mortgage loan in full. In fact, the amount that you can borrow is based on a "reverse mortgage calculator" and tied to your age, your home value, the type of loan you want, and the interest rate. The maximum reverse mortgage loan amount was increased to $625,500. You can get this money in different ways—for example, in one lump sum, as "tenure" monthly payments for as long as you live in your home, in "term" monthly payments for a set number of years, as a line-of-credit loan that you can draw on when you want to, or various other combinations of ways.

been higher—and that's true even more so today, due to a shift in reverse mortgage loan terms more commonly available in the new economy. Until 2006, Fannie purchased and held in its portfolio almost all Home Equity Conversion Mortgage loans, most of which tended to have adjustable interest rates. But once reverse mortgage loan securitization began and investors began buying them, the number of reverse mortgage loans with fixed rates shot from 3 percent to 70 percent—not necessarily because reverse mortgage loan borrowers preferred a fixed rate, but because the investors did. Over the past few years, because of concerns over the risk to taxpayers (meaning government anticipated losses due to plummeting home values, reverse mortgage defaults and foreclosures, and worries there would not be money to cover the losses), other new rules and reforms were put in place that inadvertently also caused some reverse mortgage loans to become more expensive.

The Great Recession and troubles in housing uncovered the challenges faced by reverse mortgage loan borrowers, ultimately serving as a catalyst for new rules and reforms. For example, at one point under the old rules, the position was taken that if you inherited a home from a parent or spouse who had taken out a reverse mortgage loan, and you wanted to keep the home, you had to pay off the full reverse mortgage loan balance, even if the home had dropped in value. Now, in the wake of a lawsuit by AARP and a lot of bad press, when a reverse mortgage loan becomes due following the mortgager's death and the property is transferred (by his will or by law) to his estate or heirs, that recipient can pay off the reverse mortgage loan by repaying the reverse mortgage loan balance or 95 percent of the home's then-current appraised value, whichever is less. The new rules and reforms also include additional changes to reverse mortgage loan servicing practices, requirements for lender-provided information about pre-application reverse mortgage loan counseling, new rules and reforms regarding eviction after foreclosure of a reverse mortgage loan, and permitted repayment time frames.

The "Standard" and "Hybrid"

Reverse mortgage loans have not been without other criticism. For example, only the adjustable rate reverse mortgage loans allow borrowers to withdraw their money over time. The "standard" fixed rate version requires that borrowers withdraw the full reverse mortgage loan amount up-front (whether or not they want or need all of that money all at once) and does not provide for any sort of reserve—for example, for the payment of real estate taxes and insurance. In the past, this requirement of fixed rate reverse mortgage loans has been known to cause some borrowers to end up being unable to pay their own real estate taxes, insurance, or FHA-required home repairs, a leading cause of reverse mortgage loan default and foreclosure.

More than 65 percent of reverse mortgage loan borrowers opt for the fixed rate option in order to take advantage of historically low interest rates and avoid the pitfalls of rising interest rates during their fixed income retirement years. But, particularly in the new economy, this "full loan amount" draw requirement has subjected the precious home equity of America's seniors to seemingly unnecessary risk. Moving forward, you can expect to see further changes in the types of reverse mortgage loans available, all in response to the new rules and reforms and other dynamics in the new economy. For example, a proposed "hybrid" reverse mortgage loan, allowing for an up-front, fixed rate draw, followed by subsequent adjustable rate draws, may increase the range of reverse mortgage loan options available for your retirement fresh start.

"The Saver"

Similar criticism of the relatively high-cost, up-front mortgage insurance premium fees associated with reverse mortgage loans in the new economy also resulted in the introduction of the "Saver" reverse mortgage loan product. The Saver has lower up-front fees (borrowers can save thousands of dollars because of the reduced initial mortgage insurance premium) but typically higher interest rates and other ongoing costs. Saver reverse mortgage loans also provide less money to you (about 10 percent to 18 percent less, depending on your age) than standard reverse mortgage loans. All in all, if your retirement fresh start contemplates getting a reverse mortgage loan, the Saver may be a good option if you need to borrow only a relatively small amount of money.

The Banks

Aside from new reverse mortgage loan rules, reforms, and products, the new economy has had another interesting impact on reverse mortgage loans. More particularly, several of America's largest banks, including Bank of America, MetLife, and Wells Fargo, made the decision to stop offering reverse mortgage loans altogether, indicating that perhaps in light of the new economy's challenges with home values, limited bank resources, and overwhelming needs from distressed borrowers, reverse mortgage loan products are just not worth the effort. Chalk up another one for unintended consequences.

Reverse Mortgage Loan Demographics in the New Economy

The demographic of folks who are taking out reverse mortgages loan seems to be skewing toward younger borrowers (ages 62 to

65). Younger borrowers are, likewise, making up the bulk of reverse mortgage loan delinquencies in the new economy, a trend believed to be directly related to the Great Recession and America's poor economy. In fact, these growing delinquencies have prompted new rules and reforms in assessing potential reverse mortgage loan borrowers' ability to pay their ongoing expenses, such as real estate taxes, insurance, and repairs and maintenance. With rising numbers of America's seniors expected to use reverse mortgage loans in the future, creating a more sustainable lending process has become a priority in both the industry itself and Washington.

Around 8 percent of all reverse mortgage loans are currently delinquent. Despite this increase in the number of delinquencies, most of them are, in truth, for relatively small amounts. Almost half of these delinquent borrowers owe less than $2,000. To control reverse mortgage loan defaults and foreclosures, the FHA introduced a special counseling program for defaulting reverse mortgage loan borrowers; however, the ability of these borrowers to stick to repayment plans developed through this counseling has been limited, since most are on fixed incomes.

In situations where keeping the home is no longer an option, counselors from the Department of Housing and Urban Development (HUD) are helping reverse loan mortgage borrowers transition to alternative housing. Remember, since FHA insures most reverse mortgage loans, all of this is being done with your taxpayer dollars. In fact, television advertisements for reverse mortgage loans that reference the loans as being "government insured" are somewhat misleading for older folks, as that seems to indicate that borrowers are somehow insured by America's government; in truth, the banks are the beneficiaries of FHA's promise.

As you may have already guessed, for all of the reasons discussed so far, the Consumer Financial Protection Bureau has its eye on regulating and reforming reverse mortgages, so stay tuned! For more information on reverse mortgages, check out the online video clip at www.askshario.com/reversemortgages.

Fresh Start Tips for Reverse Mortgage Loans

Here are some tips if your own retirement fresh start includes a reverse mortgage loan.

- *Shop around.* Fees vary widely. HUD has limited origination fees but not yield spread premium.

- *Don't be oversold.* Don't take out more than what you need. Favor line of credit (LOC) or periodic payments, not a lump sum. And don't be sold products you don't need (especially by brokers seeking higher commissions).

- *Only use for essentials.* The main use should be to pay off an existing mortgage, repairs, and improvements.

- *Understand.* Read the fine print. Before taking out a reverse mortgage, it is wise to ensure that you understand the terms, which may be more complicated than average. Remember, counseling is now an integral part of the reverse mortgage process—your bank is legally required to give you a list of five unrelated counseling agencies within your state along with four national intermediaries that HUD has given authority to provide counseling. This counseling is also available through a nationwide telephone network, so you'll have plenty of people to direct your questions to.

- *Think ahead.* Think through the possible pitfalls. For example, if you only plan to stay in your home for a few years, a reverse mortgage loan may not be worth the expense.

- *Compare alternatives.* Generally, if you can make traditional home mortgage loan payments or have other assets or income sources, a reverse mortgage loan is probably not the most cost-effective way for you to access funds. For many folks, a home equity line of credit, downsizing, or even renting out a room in order to make ends meet, rather than counting on having cash available from a reverse mortgage loan, may be more prudent retirement fresh start options.

- *Delay.* Put off taking out a reverse mortgage loan as long as you can to avoid outliving your home equity. The minimum reverse mortgage loan age of 62 is no longer in line with modern life expectancies.

- *Consider working with a specialist.* Contact a Certified Reverse Mortgage Professional (CRMP) or find a specialist through the National Reverse Mortgage Association (NRMA) or the AARP.

The Bottom Line

The adage that nothing is certain in this world of course holds true for your savings, investments, and retirement, and even more so under the new economy, rules, and reforms. Some financial planning is better than none at all. For most folks that means keeping it simple: diversifying among and within the five basic investment categories; maximizing your retirement vehicles; and keeping a watchful eye out for telltale signs in interest rates, inflation, tax legislation, and the new laws governing your money manager. The next chapter takes us to step 4 of your financial fresh start. It exposes the hidden challenges created by an American government determined not to let the housing bubble bring down the entire economy. As always, there are unintended consequences, but also once-in-a-lifetime opportunities you'll want to take advantage of.

CHAPTER FIVE

Step Four:
Decide If Homeownership
Is Right for You

- **What Will You Learn from This Chapter?** As the original economic trouble spot that eventually grew into an unsustainable bubble and the Great Recession, homeownership proved its uniquely powerful role in personal and national prosperity. This chapter covers the important rules and reforms that have changed the landscape of American homeownership.

- **How Will This Know-How Help You?** Knowing how to resolve a housing or home mortgage loan challenge in your favor, and take advantage of real estate opportunities in the new economy, is one of the most important pillars of your fresh start plan for financial prosperity.

As is the case with some of the topics already covered, the exact details of everybody's homeownership-relevant circumstances differ.

This chapter begins with tools for resolving homeownership and home mortgage problems and then moves on to renting and taking advantage of other real estate investment opportunities. Many of the references to your home in this chapter also apply to other types of real estate you may own, including commercial, income, and vacation properties.

Deciding If Homeownership Is Still for You

No savings, investing, and retirement fresh start would be complete without taking into consideration investing in a home, and perhaps even other real estate. Aside from that, you need to live *someplace.* You know from Chapter 1 that Americans have historically relied on the equity in their homes as a financial safety net and nest egg for big expenditures and, eventually, to fund their retirement. In fact, as shown in Figure 5-1, until recently homeownership, or more specifically home equity, comprised the majority of personal wealth for most of America's middle class. So what happened?

Your parents' or grandparents' generation generally worked hard to pay off their home mortgage loan so they could own their homes free and clear. Because that approach to homeownership worked well for hundreds of millions of people over several decades, it seems reasonable to call it a proven strategy. In fact, about 30 percent of Americans still own their homes free and clear. On the other hand, more recently some modern-day American homeowners seem to have borrowed as much money as possible against home equity, an approach that, unfortunately, did not end well for many folks. Almost a third of all homeowners with a mortgage are underwater or have little or no equity in their homes, which isn't really *owning* a home at all. As a result, in addition to the many other outcomes of the

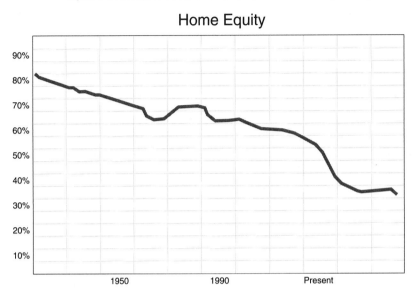

Figure 5-1. Average American's home equity has decreased significantly.

Great Recession, more and more folks are questioning the entire concept of homeownership, when, perhaps instead, they should be reevaluating the wisdom of borrowing against their homes.

How, then, does homeownership now play into your own savings, investment, and retirement fresh start plan? The tips and tools in this chapter will help you in these important fresh start choices. We'll begin with fresh start strategies if you're currently in a tough homeownership situation. But feel free to skip to sections applicable to you.

Facing Tough Truths: Foreclosures Alternatives and Getting on with Your Life

If your fresh start includes figuring out a challenging housing or home mortgage loan situation, you are not alone. More than 6 million Americans are in default or foreclosure. Another 4 million folks have sadly already lost their homes. The subject of foreclosure can fill an entire book, but the following quick overview will give you a great fresh start starting point. So, if this situation describes you, what should you do?

The first caveat if you are facing foreclosure is don't panic. This is not your father's foreclosure; nowadays, there isn't the same stigma attached. Calling your bank is advisable as it allows you to gather the information that you will need to know in order to begin fleshing out your options. Among the reasons some people are in tough housing and mortgage loan situations in the new economy in the first place is because they didn't take the time to educate themselves before making their home purchase, mortgage loan, or refinance decisions.

Another reason to call the bank is that by doing so, your bank becomes responsible for complying with certain new rules and reforms. For example, several states have new rules and reforms requiring banks to mediate certain foreclosure cases. Mediation puts you and a bank representative in a room with a neutral mediator to see if you can work things out (typically agreeing to one of the foreclosure alternatives I'll discuss shortly). You can learn more about mediation from the video clip at www.askshario.com/mediation.

When you call your bank, be sure to ask:

- *Who owns or guarantees your mortgage?* If it's Fannie Mae or Freddie Mac, check out the Making Home Affordable website at www.mha.gov for new initiatives you may be eligible and qualify for. If you have a Federal Housing Administration (FHA) home mortgage loan, check out www.fha.gov. If it's another investor, ask about any restrictions contained in the servicer's contract with the investor and other legal agreements, since those restrictions may impact how the bank can help you. One of these restrictions, commonly referred to as the "net present value" test that servicers must use to determine whether a foreclosure alternative is in an investor's best interest, will be discussed shortly. For more about the bank-servicer-investor relationship and these types of contracts, also see the online Appendix.

• *How much money is due now and what is the breakdown?* How much more money will be accruing and when? It will be helpful for you to know the breakdown of what the bank says you owe because some of these line items are negotiable. This information will also allow you to determine whether errors have been made in the calculations.

• *How do the bank's process and your state laws work?* In other words, how much time do you have to come up with a solution before the bank actually takes back your home?

• *What are the foreclosure alternatives the bank is offering to borrowers, in general, nowadays?* Does the person that you are speaking with think that other options may become available soon? What are most other borrowers in your situation doing? And what can you expect in terms of the process, requirements, and time frames for each? At a minimum, make sure that you understand the most common foreclosure alternatives and which ones are available to you: Alternatives including mortgage modification, refinance, deed in lieu, and short sale are explained in detail later in this chapter. Note that the banks and Freddie, Fannie, and FHA are constantly changing the parameters for these program alternatives *and* devising new ways to try to keep folks in their homes. So if you don't qualify for the program you want or there doesn't seem to be an alternative that fits your situation, you may want to wait a few weeks and try calling the bank again.

If your own home mortgage loan is in default or foreclosure, it goes without saying that reading everything you get in the mail from your bank is imperative. Now is probably also a good time to read the documents that you signed when you got the loan and, in particular, your promissory note and mortgage agreement.

If you do not already know, it is well worth your time to learn whether you live in a *judicial* state, where a judge rules on foreclosures, or a *trustee* (or *nonjudicial*) state, where there is no judge involved. These differences and what they mean for you are covered for you in the sidebar opposite.

Foreclosure Alternatives and the New Reforms

As mentioned earlier, four common alternatives to foreclosure are (1) mortgage modification, (2) refinancing, (3) short sale, and (4) deed in lieu of foreclosure.

1. Mortgage Modification

Mortgage modification is a process where the bank agrees to change the terms you originally agreed to in your home mortgage loan. Mortgage modifications can involve, for example, changing the interest rate to a higher or lower rate or an adjustable rate to a fixed rate; changing the manner in which the interest rate is calculated; or lengthening or shortening the repayment or amortization period. Generally, the purpose of a modification is to make the payment more affordable.

2. Refinance

Refinancing involves replacing an existing mortgage loan with a new one. Reasons to refinance include getting different mortgage loan terms,

One-Minute Mentor:
What Is the Difference Between a Judicial State and a Trustee (or Nonjudicial) State?

A mortgage loan is documented by two primary agreements:

1. The promissory note is essentially an IOU from you to the bank.

2. The mortgage, which in trustee states is called a deed of trust, is essentially the collateral (your home) you post to ensure that you repay the promissory note.

The mortgage or deed-of-trust foreclosure process works differently in each state, but two methods are the most common:

1. *Judicial Foreclosures* involve the sale of the property under the supervision of a court. Typically, the bank first files a "complaint," the homeowner files an "answer" containing a defense or counterclaims, and eventually a judge rules on whether or not the foreclosure proceeds. If the ruling is in the bank's favor, the property is sold at auction (now done online in many areas) and the proceeds from the sale go to pay off the promissory note (which is essentially the IOU from you to your bank). Anything left over after paying other qualified creditors goes to the borrower.

2. *Nonjudicial Foreclosures* are conducted by the bank when it is authorized by a "power of sale" clause in the deed of trust. A "notice of default" is filed and served on the homeowner. If the homeowner does not cure the default (or file bankruptcy), the property is sold by the bank at auction. Nonjudicial foreclosures are therefore generally much faster and cheaper than foreclosures by judicial sale. A few states impose additional procedural requirements; however, in most states, the only government official involved in a nonjudicial foreclosure is the county recorder.

such as a better interest rate or a shorter amortization or repayment period (e.g., fifteen years instead of thirty); consolidating two or more mortgages or other obligations into one mortgage loan; reducing the monthly payment; or reducing another risk, such as switching from an adjustable interest rate loan to a fixed interest rate loan.

3. Short Sale

A short sale involves the sale of your home for less money than you owe the bank for your mortgage loan and an agreement by your bank to accept that lesser amount to repay your mortgage loan in order to avoid foreclosure. If you have other assets, the bank may want you to use your other assets to pay some or all of the "deficiency"—the difference between what you owe on your mortgage loan and what the bank agrees to accept from the sale. Negotiating how the bank will report a short sale on your credit report is important as well. For more on short sales, see the online video at www.askshario.com/shortsales1 and www.askshario.com/shortsales2. Many banks are even offering money incentives for folks to agree to a short sale or a deed in lieu, as discussed next.

4. Deed in Lieu of Foreclosure

A deed in lieu of foreclosure involves transferring title to your home to the bank in order to satisfy your mortgage loan and avoid foreclosure. As is the case with a short sale, the deficiency and how the deed in lieu will be reflected on your credit report are part of the usual negotiation process.

These foreclosure alternatives themselves are nothing new. What is new are the various manners in which each of these foreclosure alternatives have been adopted by the government (Fannie, Freddie, and FHA) and the various banks and servicers and the new rules and reforms affecting their foreclosure alternative programs and practices. For example, President Barack Obama's Making Home Affordable (MHA) initiative, which covers Fannie and Freddie home mortgage loans, includes several programs, among them HAMP, HARP, and HAFA—that use these foreclosure alternatives:

1. *Home Affordable Modification Program (HAMP)* has specific loan modification guidelines. To qualify for a HAMP modification, your loan has to have been originated before January 1, 2009; it has to be a first mortgage and the property has to be your primary residence; your loan balance can't be more than $729,750; and your "debt-to-income" ratio can't be more than 31 percent (meaning that your loan payment, real estate taxes, insurance, and condo or HOA fees can't be more than 31 percent of your gross monthly income). In calculating how your loan will be modified, HAMP uses what's called a "waterfall" approach: first, reducing your interest rate to as little as 2 percent; then, if necessary, extending your loan term to up to forty years; and then, if still necessary, considering principal forbearance (which essentially tacks part of the loan on to the very end so that your payments for now are lower). Homeowners who make their payments on time under HAMP are eligible for up to $1,000 of principal reduction payments each year for up to five years. But remember, these criteria are constantly being tweaked, so if at first you're not eligible or don't qualify, even if you don't like the foreclosure alternative you are offered, try, try again.

2. *Home Affordable Refinance Program (HARP) and HARP 2.0,* like the HAMP modification, is one of the two original Making Home Affordable foreclosure alternatives and has also been repeatedly tweaked, most recently with the

REALITY CHECK: Are Your Homeownership Challenges Temporary or More Than That?

Knowledge is power. Once you know the worst-case scenario, you can be more prepared for it and less afraid of it. After you have the facts and your bank knows that you're working on a solution, it's time to take a long, hard look at yourself. How did you get into this situation in the first place? Is the problem temporary, the result of a onetime medical issue or short-term job loss that caused you to get behind? Or is it more permanent, caused, for instance, by a divorce that took you from two incomes to one? Or did you just get in over your head? In order for a modification or refinance to work, you need to decide if you can afford the modification or refinance payments. And even if you can, do you want that pressure? In other words, should you be figuring out a long-term way to stay in your home, or are you better off with a short-term solution so that you can have time to scale back and find a more affordable place to live? Are there other factors such as a second mortgage, co-owner or co-borrower, or bad credit you need to consider? Are the taxes current, and are there issues with any of your other payment obligations? Do you own more than one property? Are you behind on those other loans, too? Is the property your primary residence? Have you tried to refinance, modify, or sell before? Are you working? Should you be considering bankruptcy? More than half of all home mortgage loan modifications end in default again, in part because the homeowner does not think through these considerations ahead of time. Folks are getting a second chance at a fresh start. The likelihood of a third chance is slim to none, so learn from the mistakes others are making and avoid the same pitfalls. In most instances, you will get only one chance at a foreclosure alternative fresh start, meaning it's imperative that you approach it realistically and get it right.

introduction of HARP 2.0. Among the changes, HARP 2.0 removes the requirement that your home not be more than 25 percent underwater in order to qualify (the very first version of this program allowed only 5 percent negative equity, a main reason it didn't work). HARP 2.0 also reduces the cost to refinance for borrowers willing to get loans with terms of twenty years or less, and it waives the usual waiting periods for borrowers with a prior bankruptcy or foreclosure on their record. To qualify under HARP 2.0, you need to be current on your mortgage for at least the last six months and cannot have missed more than one payment in the past year. As with HAMP, this program is continually changing, so be sure to check this book's online Appendix for updates.

3. *Home Affordable Foreclosure Alternatives (HAFA)* includes two options: a short sale and a deed in lieu of foreclosure. The HAFA program was introduced some time after the original Making Home Affordable HAMP and HARP programs.

In addition to these aforementioned foreclosure alternative programs, MHA also includes a limited principal reduction program and a program to help borrowers resolve challenges with second mortgages.

When the Obama administration originally announced Making Home Affordable, HAMP and HARP were planned to help 9 million Americans. Actual success rates have been significantly lower. However, Making Home Affordable was successful in serving as a prototype for banks developing their own "proprietary" mortgage modification, short sale, deed in lieu of foreclosure, and similar foreclosure alternatives. Additionally, various settlements, investigations, and lawsuits have essentially forced banks to offer still more foreclosure alternatives. These proprietary foreclosure alternatives offered by various banks continue to evolve, and the eligibility and qualification criteria are likewise being tweaked. More resources to help you find and access programs your own bank is offering can be found in the online Appendix.

In summary, if you are not eligible or *don't* qualify for a Making Home Affordable solution, your bank may have other solutions for which you may qualify. And even if you do qualify for an MHA solution, your bank may offer even better terms with its own proprietary programs, so be sure to ask. For more about Making Home Affordable, check out the online video clip at www.askshario. com/MHA.

What Is Net Present Value?

Aside from the legal contracts between banks, servicers, and investors (as discussed previously), how do the banks decide which modification, short sale, or other foreclosure alternative requests will or will not be approved? Banks generally base their decisions regarding foreclosure alternatives on whether the net present value of granting your request is more or less than the net present value of foreclosing.

The term *net present value* simply means the current value of future cash flow minus costs. Applied to your home mortgage loan default or foreclosure, net present value means the dollar amount that your bank will recover once your home mortgage loan is paid off (either by foreclosing and selling your home or otherwise), minus all of the costs the bank will have to pay to get to that point and adjusted for other factors and variables such as the amount of time that will take.

For example, the bank may calculate that it will probably recover more money in the long run if it approves a foreclosure alternative request than if it decides to foreclose on the homeowner immediately; in this case, most banks will approve the option with the higher net present value, which is the foreclosure alternative request. In fact, oftentimes the contracts between banks, servicers, and investors legally require that these decisions be based on net present value.

There are several inherent problems with net present value (NPV), not the least of which are the facts that banks use different formulas to compute NPV and all formulas, by definition, include guesstimates and assumptions that are not always accurate or equally applicable. There are wide differences in input data and other industry-related data referenced by the formulas.

Perhaps the biggest frustration with the use of net present value by banks in this context has been the lack of explanation provided to borrowers. NPV calculations are done by computer, based on information from a variety of sources that may or may not be current and correct (as they say, garbage in means garbage out). As a result (until the new rules and reforms), a modification or short sale approval or denial, for example, was communicated to the borrower simply as a "yes" or "failed NPV" with no further explanation or opportunity. This communication gap has had unfortunate consequences for many homeowners who, had they better understood the role of net present value, may have been able to show their banks how they can increase the NPV of granting their foreclosure alternative request. The concept of basing the bank's decision on net present value is not, in and of itself, entirely unreasonable. After all, a somewhat uniform procedure that attempts to objectively balance bank, servicer, investor, and borrower interests is both necessary and appropriate for evaluating foreclosure alternative requests. But it benefits everyone when banks and borrowers can work together to ensure that a foreclosure alternative achieves the higher NPV over simply foreclosing.

In response to this frustration and the potential missed opportunity to help borrowers to better prepare their case for a foreclosure alternative request, the U.S. Treasury has launched a Web-based tool at www.CheckMyNPV.com to enable homeowners to calculate their own net present value. The site utilizes the NPV formulas used for HAMP modifications. So, if you have a Fannie or Freddie home mortgage loan, this tool is a perfect fit for you. Using it before you apply for a foreclosure alternative will allow you to make the best possible case for yourself and to provide your bank with the NPV calculations you did yourself to support your request. But even if your loan is not with Fannie or Freddie, tools like this one help give you a much better idea of whether your short sale or modification request looks good on paper and what, if anything, you can do to make it look better. This is also a wonderful tool for folks who have already been denied a request, providing them an opportunity to go back and look at the reasons why and address them.

If your homeownership fresh start includes asking for a foreclosure alternative, it is also imperative that you get very aggressive with your own income and expenses. If you need to get a part-time job in order to prove that you will be able to pay a modified mortgage, then do it. If you need to get rid of your kids' iPhones so you can get your debt-to-income ratios down, then do it! There are plenty of stories about folks who, literally, lost their home because expenses like smartphone bills threw their ratios out of whack. You have the opportunity to learn from their mistakes. Applying for a foreclosure alternative is not simply a matter of filling in the blanks on paperwork and mailing it in. It's up to you to know exactly what your bank will be looking for in order to approve your request, and it's up to you to tweak your application (along with your lifestyle) to make sure you get what you ask for. Expecting to simply be approved without doing the legwork up-front to make sure you meet the criteria is an unrealistic expectation.

Beyond MHA

In addition to Making Home Affordable, there are other government-related initiatives that may be of interest to you. They include FHA Short Refinances (for folks who are underwater) and Hope for Homeowners. There are even some more creative programs like Fannie's Lease for Deed, which allows you to give your home back to your bank and then rent it back as a tenant.

Lease for Deed may be a fresh start foreclosure alternative that works for you if you can't afford to keep your home but don't want to move. To qualify, the home must be your primary residence; you need to have made at least three mortgage loan payments and be less than twelve payments behind; you cannot have a bankruptcy or other liens; and you have to be able to verify your income. Many banks are experimenting with similar lease-for-deed-type programs, so if this option sounds like something that would work for you, it pays to ask if your bank has a program like it.

Fresh Start Help If Your Housing Challenge Is Related to Under- or Unemployment

In the new economy, if your employment circumstances are creating problems paying your mortgage, your first line of defense is to go to your bank and ask for an unemployment forbearance. Forbearance is a period of time during which the bank will allow you to not pay your mortgage loan, or pay a lower amount, after which you will typically need to eventually pay back the full sums due. During this period, the bank agrees to "forbear" from enforcing its legal rights (such as foreclosure).

Initially banks and servicers were offering unemployment forbearances for three or four months. Now, many offer unemployment forbearances for up to twelve months.

Another helpful resource is the Hardest Hit Fund, which dedicates $7.6 billion in federal funds to assist unemployed or underemployed Americans facing home mortgage loan–related challenges.

Local HUD-approved housing counselors can fill you in on even more resources available if you're struggling with an unemployment or underemployment situation. And check out this online video clip www.askshario.com/helpforunemployed.

Is Refinancing Your Answer?

With interest rates at all-time lows, refinancing can resolve a variety of issues. For example, by negotiating for a lower interest rate, you can reduce your monthly payments; another example is to reduce the term of your mortgage, say, from thirty years to twenty years. Whatever your reason for refinancing, you need to know where to go, how to shop, and how much to refinance (in other words, all or just part of your outstanding debt). Thanks to low interest rates and new programs such as HARP 2.0, refinancing in the new economy is a wonderful opportunity to save big money. Even if you have already refinanced, it may make sense to refinance again.

However, all the ads for "all-time low rates" can be misleading, because very few folks qualify for the very best rates. Here are some tips that can save you thousands of dollars.

Compare Apples to Apples

Compare interest rates, fees, and amortization terms. Also compare requirements, likelihood of approval, and timeline to close. The average cost for somebody with decent credit to refinance was historically around 2 percent, but with the cost of the new rules and reforms, 3 percent to 4 percent is now more common. Add one-quarter point if your loan is in the million-dollar or more range.

Pay Down the Loan to Not Be Underwater

If being underwater is preventing you from refinancing and if you can afford to pay down your current loan (and you plan to stay in your home for the long term), it may make sense for you to do so. This is called a "cash-in refinance." The lower interest rate can even save you more money than a principal reduction.

Restart the Clock

But think about whether or not you wish to restart the amortization period on your loan. In other words, if your loan will be paid off in another five years, do you really want to reset it and be paying for another fifteen, twenty, or thirty years again?

Evaluate Your Current Bank vs. a New Bank

Your current bank may waive some documents, credit, and other requirements. Many banks are offering incentives. Other times, you'll find new banks will do more to win your business, particularly for good higher-end borrowers or those willing to move other accounts over. Terms are more negotiable than you may think! Don't forget about other banks with which you have current relationships, perhaps for your business, car loan, or other loans and accounts. Shop at least three different banks for a refinance, and don't forget the smaller community and regional banks. These guys often offer flat-fee refinances or will roll in the costs or provide other incentives for you.

Evaluate Mortgage Broker vs. Bank Direct Options

In theory, mortgage brokers have access to more mortgage loans options than a typical banker, so they can find you the best deal. In practice, as many people learned, mortgage brokers often find you instead the deal that will make them the most money. There are also benefits to homeowners building relationships directly with banks and cutting out potential middleman fees. Generally, folks who can go directly to a bank do and should, but it makes sense to shop both alternatives.

Calculate Your Break-Even Point

It still costs money to refinance. Your loan officer can help you do the math. Your break-even point is the point at which the amount of money you will save each month on the new loan mortgage monthly payment adds up to more than the amount of money that you will spend in order to refinance. Most folks will find that happens at about year three. For more guidance, check out the video clips at www.askshario.com/refinancing1 and www.askshario.com/refinancing2.

Getting Help If You're UnderWater

Being underwater recently began to outpace unemployment as the leading cause for default and foreclosure. If you owe your bank more money than your home is worth, you may simply want to cut your losses with a short sale or deed in lieu of foreclosure. But if you live in a recourse state (see below) and have other assets, your bank may expect that you pony up some cash, too, in order to help absorb some of the loss that your bank will incur. If that works for you, great. If not, perhaps you're better off staying put rather than giving up and becoming a renter, at least for the time being.

Deficiency Judgments and Recourse

As explained earlier, the *deficiency* in a mortgage loan foreclosure is the difference between the amount of money that you owe your bank and the amount of money the bank is paid when your home is sold. Depending upon which state you live in, you may be legally liable to repay the deficiency to the bank even after your home is foreclosed. There are three types of states where mortgage loan deficiencies are concerned:

1. *Recourse.* In a recourse state, you are liable for the deficiency.

2. *Nonrecourse.* In a nonrecourse state you are not liable for the deficiency.

3. *Hybrid.* In a hybrid state you are liable for the deficiency under certain circumstances. For example, in some states you are liable for the deficiency on an investment property, but not on your primary residence.

So what can you do if it looks as if your bank is pursuing you for a deficiency judgment? The first option is to try to negotiate a settlement. You may have some leverage if your bank believes that it will be difficult or costly to find and collect from your assets. Or perhaps there are laws that you believe your bank has breached that may serve as defenses. If you try to negotiate a deficiency, expect your bank to ask for current financial statements in order to independently verify what assets you do and do not have and which of your assets, if any, may be exempt from a deficiency (for example, Social Security, unemployment, and Veterans Administration benefits or disability checks).

Your bank will also refer to your initial loan application and the financial information you provided at that time. (If you happen to have other accounts or assets with the same bank pursuing you for a deficiency, remember the documents you signed when you opened those accounts may also allow your bank to tap them if you default on your home mortgage loan.) Some of the factors influencing whether your bank is likely to settle include the amount of time and money the bank believes will be required in order to collect from you, the bank's potential exposure if it loses, and the likelihood that you may file bankruptcy and that other creditors will be awarded from the assets the bank is seeking. In the new economy, banks are also often influenced by their own overall financial condition and reserves, as well as issues and challenges they are currently dealing with, including regulators and public perception.

Unfortunately, banks nowadays are also often selling deficiency judgments to more aggressive debt collectors. This cottage industry is growing by leaps and bounds. If your deficiency judgment happens to be purchased by a debt collector, the chances that you will be aggressively pursued increases tenfold. And remember, it's not just first mortgage holders that can pursue you. In fact, second mortgage holders are far less likely to be paid in full when your home sells and thus tend to pursue deficiency judgments even more.

For more information on deficiency judgments, see the online video clips at www.askshario.com/avoiddeficiencyjudgment and www.askshario.com/deficiencyjudgment.

Bank Help If You're Underwater and Want to Stay in Your Home

The most sought-after solution for folks who are underwater is asking the bank for a principal reduction. That makes sense since a principal reduction will immediately put you back into a positive equity position. But the truth is, principal reductions are rare (in large part because the net present value test, explained earlier, favors foreclosure). One solution that may be available, and on paper can do almost as much good, is a refinance that reduces your interest rate and monthly payment.

Self-Help If You're Underwater and Want to Stay in Your Home

Because there are strong emotions and other factors tied to owning your home, the majority of folks who are underwater actually still want to stay in their homes. If you're one of them, you may be wondering what you can do to get your home value back up above what you owe the bank. Being underwater involves a two-part equation: The first part is how much money your home is worth; the second is how much money you owe the bank. Solutions for getting yourself out from underwater attack your negative equity from both of these angles.

First, there are things you can do to improve the value of your home. In the category of home improvements are:

- *Façades.* Exterior replacement projects routinely reward owners with a big bang for the buck. Façade work, walkways, and landscaping especially improve curb appeal. Done cost-effectively but smartly, these projects can improve your home value by as much as 5 percent.

- *Bath and Kitchen Surfaces.* Kitchen and bath "face-lifts" likewise improve the overall impression that your home gives in terms of value. There's no need to gut it all, just redo surfaces, replace hardware and faucets, and don't spare the paint and new floor coverings.

- *Usable Square Footage.* Home prices are calculated based on usable square footage. So if your home has an outdoor area or perhaps even a garage or carport that can be legally covered, enclosed, or cost efficiently converted to be actually usable square footage, do it!

The second part of solving your negative equity problem involves decreasing what you owe the bank. This, likewise, happens naturally as you pay down your mortgage loan each month. But there are some actions you can take to speed up the process.

- *Cash-In Refinance.* Of course, if you have an interest rate that's higher than current rates and are able to refinance into a lower rate loan, that may be a good option. If you can do a shorter-term amortization period, even better. Being underwater, you will most likely need to bring money to the closing table.

- *Mortgage Repayments.* If refinancing is not an option, try paying more toward your monthly mortgage when you can. This may be an especially appropriate option if you are near retirement. Accelerating your principal payment will result in huge savings down the line. Adding as little as $300 a month to a monthly mortgage loan payment on a $300,000 loan at around 6.25 percent can save you ten years of mortgage payments (which adds up to $83,000). If paying down your mortgage faster is part of your homeownership fresh start, be careful to send a separate check and note in the memo section of your check that it is for an additional principal prepayment. And keep good records. Also, be sure your mortgage doesn't have a prepayment penalty.

- *Biweekly Payments.* Even if you can't prepay any principal, maybe you can switch to biweekly payments instead of paying once a month. Check with your lender first, to be sure it allows this type of payment plan. Biweekly payments will cut several years, and lots of interest cost, off of your loan, too.

For more information on all these approaches, check out the video clips at www.askshario.com/underwater1 and www.askshario.com/underwater2.

Easy Ways to Know If You're Better Off Renting

This chapter, ultimately, is about deciding if homeownership is right for you. In truth, 90 percent of Americans, the vast majority, are able to pay their home mortgage loans. Nevertheless, *everybody* is facing some of the many consequences of foreclosure, including a soft national real estate market (albeit with some pockets of markets that are already doing well again), drops in home values (by as much as

40 percent to 60 percent in the harder hit states), and the prospect of several more years of the same in some areas. As such, you may be a potential first-time homebuyer, a move-up buyer, or even someone who suffered a foreclosure and is wondering if you should buy or if it is better to rent under the new economy rules and reforms.

Foreclosures and fear of buying are definitely tipping the scales, causing more folks than before to choose renting over buying. Tighter credit is also an issue. Banks are already beginning to conform to guidelines akin to the new Qualified Residential Mortgage (QRM) rules and reforms discussed in Chapter 2. Using the new economy's minimum FICO scores, maximum loan-to-value ratios, and the requirement that folks who went through a foreclosure, short sale, or deed in lieu must wait before they can buy again, many Americans will not be able to qualify for a home mortgage loan any time soon.

Consequently, millions of people have become renters by choice or necessity. Rental vacancies in America are at an all-time low, driving rental rates up. Homeownership has long been associated with the "American Dream" and renting considered a last resort, but that perception is quickly changing. Demographic shifts, with traditional *renters* taking advantage of the new economy's mantra of "now's a good time to buy" and traditional *owners* foreclosed or fearful and now renting, are interesting new economy dynamics. For more on that subject, check out the video clips at www.askshario. com/rentorbuy1 and www.askshario.com/rentorbuy2. And for more tips if you decide that renting is a better choice for you, check out the video clip at www.askshario.com/renttips.

Is Your Home a Good Investment?

The strictly mathematical calculations for rational folks deciding whether to buy a home or rent and invest the same money elsewhere begins with a consideration of the potential return on a financial investment in homeownership vs. other investment vehicles, such as stocks, bonds, certificates of deposit, and the like. Of course, every situation varies, but a quick look at average annual returns on home investments during the three decades preceding the real estate bubble vs. traditional alternative investments reveals an 8.6 percent return on home investments and a 13.4 percent on stocks.

But this does not account for one significant advantage that investing in your home has over other types of investments—namely, the ability to finance your home purchase at relatively reasonable rates (which most folks cannot do with other investments, as I'll discuss in more detail shortly). This advantage necessitates the long-term nature of an investment in your home, mainly because you are not actually paying notable principal on your home loan until some years into the loan.

In fact, the next sidebar explains how, during the first five years of your homeownership, about 80 percent of your monthly mortgage loan payment goes toward interest. It takes twenty years before a typical borrower pays more principal each month than interest. Once you've paid all of this interest for all of these years, you can easily wind up spending three times the purchase price of your home, particularly if you also factor in real estate taxes, homeowner's insurance, ongoing maintenance, and those bigger cost repairs.

Other Factors to Consider

So, if homeownership does not return as much money as other investments like stocks, and if it can actually cost you much more than originally meets the eye, why invest your hard-earned money in owning a home? For starters, there is more to the financial

Most of Your Initial Monthly Home Mortgage Loan Payments Go Toward Interest, Not Principal

Number of Years That You Pay Your Home Mortgage Loan	Approximate Percentage of Your Monthly Payments That Will Go Toward Interest
0 to 5	80%
6 to 10	70%
11 to 15	60%
16 to 20	50%
21 to 25	35%
26 to 30	10%

equation than just that. For example, home values are much less volatile than stocks, and owning a home enhances your investment diversification. Also, as we've touched on, since you are able to finance homeownership, but not necessarily other investments, consider the fact that even if you earn only 3 percent a year, you are earning that 3 percent on the full value of your home, even though you only invested a much smaller down payment from your own pocket. And, since your home is part consumable, you would have to spend money *somewhere* in order to live.

Also, comparing the return on investment in your home to the return on investments in stocks and bonds and the like, over the same period, neglects other important aspects of homeownership. How do you factor in the stability of having a roof over your head and other comforts that owning your own home carries? (For example, children generally do better in school when their family owns the home they live in.) Furthermore, the alternative to owning your home, namely, renting, carries zero return on investment. Of course, there are also tax benefits to owning your own home.

For many folks, the fact that they might be able to earn a better return by investing their money someplace other than their home is not even relevant since many people do not have the self-discipline to actually do this kind of investing.

In fact, homeowners have historically been worth about 40 percent more than renters. Fast-forward to your ultimate goal, which is ensuring that you have sufficient funds to retire on time and in the manner you want. At the end of the day, of 23 million households headed by someone over age 65 today, 80 percent own their own home and 65 percent own their home free and clear with an average of $100,000 equity. For many Americans who do not have a savings plan (and the statistics show that most Americans do not), owning a home is essentially a forced savings account and is as good as it gets for building savings … and it ain't so bad.

The moral is that comparing the return you receive on owning your home vs. investing the same money elsewhere is simply not comparing apples with apples. And, as is the case with your personal finances in general, at the end of the day, deciding whether homeownership is for you is more about "personal" than it is about "finances." For most folks, the question is not whether they should own their own home, but rather whether (given the troubles in real estate) they should own their own home *now*?

How Can You Know *When* It's a Good Time to Buy?

If you do decide to buy a home, how do you know when to buy and how do you make sure you buy your home well? Relative to the more personal considerations, determining whether it makes sense to buy or sell a home at any given point in time (i.e., the prices of homes now and whether they will go up or down moving forward) is far less subjective.

Everything You Need to Know About Real Estate Indicators

Just as you may look to gross domestic product or cost of living in order to gauge The America Company's well-being, so too can you look to proven indicators to assess your local real estate market's well-being. Most of these indicators will show you numbers by geographic region and type of property, with year to date, month over month, and year over year comparisons, and for the primary U.S. cities referred to as "Metropolitan Statistical Areas" nearest to your own. In addition to the actual numbers, you also want to look at patterns and trends in your area, price ranges, and property types. If you are facing foreclosure, these same tools can be used to help you decide if you want to stay or go. Some of the more common real estate indicators include home sales, home prices, and home foreclosures.

Home Sales

There are plenty of resources available to help you get a handle on what's happening with America's home sales. Strong home sales absorb supply or inventory, which eventually causes prices to increase. Unfortunately, the reverse is also true. The National Association of Realtors, for example, tracks and produces several indicators, including the Pending Home Sales Index. This index is released during the first week of each month and is based on signed home purchase contracts for existing single-family homes, condos, and co-ops (in other words, this index does not count new construction home sales by builders).

The Pending Home Sales Index is considered a "leading indicator" because it helps to predict *actual* home sales since pending home sales generally become existing home sales one or two months later.

Around the twenty-fifth day of each month, the National Association of Realtors also releases its Existing Home Sales information, which includes the sales volume and median and average prices for actual sales of existing homes.

Home Prices

The National Association of Realtors also releases its Metropolitan Median Home Prices and Affordability Index each quarter. And Standard and Poor's Case-Shiller Home Price Report is released the last Tuesday of each month. The S&P indicators also reveal the percentage of cash sales and sales to investors. An issue that has been plaguing many Americans is that, notwithstanding the fact that home sales have been increasing, the majority of home sales involve distressed homes (in default or foreclosure), so home prices in many regions have still been going down. If you're buying or selling a home that's not distressed, it's important to look at home price indicators that exclude distressed sales, too.

Home Default and Foreclosures

Because homes in default or foreclosure typically end up as homes for sale at below normal prices, either as short sales or REOs (which stands for properties that are "real estate owned" by the bank, typically after a foreclosure), watching home default and foreclosure indicators will help you predict what will happen next in home prices. Areas with high foreclosure levels also tend to reflect high discounted purchase prices and rental demand. Among the many resources for this information, the RealtyTrac indicators are easily available and understandable.

Other indicators from other resources, including CoreLogic and LPS, can be tapped for real estate information relevant to your homeownership and real estate investing fresh start. More about each of these indicators, including current updates and what they mean to you, may be found in the online Appendix.

Real Estate Rules of Thumb

In addition to the above-mentioned real estate indicators, there are long-proven "rules of thumb" to serve as helpful tools in your fresh start decision making about whether to buy or rent. For example, the "rent-to-own ratio" reflects that you're better off renting if home purchase prices in your area are more than fifteen times the annual rent for comparable homes (or, conversely, you're better off buying if home prices are less than fifteen times annual rent). Likewise, the "income-to-price ratio" provides that you should not spend more than three times your annual income to buy your home. And the plus or minus 30 percent of income ratio historically utilized by lenders is a good rule of thumb to follow, meaning that you should not spend more than about a third of your income for housing. According to these rules of thumb, it is now cheaper to rent than own in about 80 percent of America's cities.

In terms of when to buy, there's one more interesting historical number you may want to factor into your homeownership fresh start plan: Home values have historically dropped for six years following a major financial crisis. This is not merely coincidence. Home values increase as homebuyer incomes increase, which of course only happens when employment stabilizes and folks get more comfortable spending money. Had Americans paid heed to historical homebuying "rules of thumb," the real estate bubble may never have happened in the first place.

Factors in Flux

Notwithstanding the indicators and rules of thumb, there are some factors unique to home values in the new economy. For example, those states that experienced the biggest gains during the bubble, and areas that have experienced severe employment problems since then, still have unique hurdles to overcome. These and other variables that impact home values remain in flux. The following explanations will help you consider which dynamics apply to home values in your own area.

Defaults, Foreclosures, and REOs

Perhaps most significant is the disposition of millions of homes in shadow inventory, much of which will sell at the 20 percent to 30 percent discount typically associated with distressed real estate. Shadow inventory is property in the process of being taken over by the bank but is not on the market yet, which means it is not showing up in the statistics. All in all, more than 6 million borrowers are behind on their payments or in foreclosure, representing one in eight residential mortgages. States with the highest percentages of noncurrent loans—which combines foreclosures and delinquencies—include Florida, Mississippi, Nevada, New Jersey, and Illinois. Clearly, real estate markets with lower default and foreclosure rates will fare better.

Pent-Up Supply and Demand vs. Inventory

With more than 40 million multigenerational households sharing space today and many first-time and move-up buyers on the sidelines waiting to get comfortable and be able to qualify for a home mortgage loan, pent-up demand will eventually work in favor of the real estate recovery. Reduction in new construction is likewise a temporary factor. Conversely, millions of folks are waiting for their home value to recover in order to downsize, relocate, or retire. Anytime you hear that an area has more than six months of housing inventory, don't be surprised to see home sales take longer and home prices to drop a bit.

Negative Equity

Nationally, about a third of American homeowners with a mortgage are at or near being underwater on their homes. Areas with higher negative equity are where home values tend to have dropped the most and are most susceptible to home mortgage loan defaults and foreclosures. Markets with lower negative equity rates will fare relatively better.

Special Demand and Value Recovery

Likewise, home values in some markets with unique special demand will appreciate quicker relative to others in the coming years. For example, the Miami, Florida, condominium market, once considered to be one of the worst in America, has been steadily climbing, until finally reaching a 54 percent increase. With the uncertainty that you see in economies around the world, foreign condominium buyers (many paying cash!) still view American real estate as a safe investment and benefit from favorable currency exchange rates, to boot.

Home Price Range Micros

Middle- and lower-income homes and homeowners will continue taking the biggest hit. On the flip side, this situation will continue creating the best opportunities for homebuyers and investors.

Unemployment

Despite all the efforts in Washington to fight unemployment, almost 13 million Americans are still officially unemployed. Markets with stable employers will fare better.

The Unexpected

There is always the possibility that something no one could have ever predicted will occur. As an example, no one predicted the robo-signer debacle that delayed foreclosures for over a year, and, some say, caused countless more foreclosures. And folks now know to expect unintended consequences in real estate and real estate finance, stemming from the new rules and reforms.

Property Type Micros

Some property types may experience more drag for longer. For example, condominiums may face excessive association fees as a result of foreclosures and some owners not paying. That situation is usually a turn off for potential buyers, which can keep sales slow and prices down.

Fresh Start Opportunities: Investing in Vacation Home or Real Estate Rental Property

Unless your last name is Trump, the fresh start rental investment opportunity for you may likely be in single-family homes or smaller mom-and-pop-type properties that have yet to appreciate and are off the radar screens of the big investors. Maybe now's a good time for you to invest in that vacation home you've always wanted. When they spot good values, lots of folks make earlier purchases of the home they plan to retire to eventually, then simply rent it out for now. Thanks to folks displaced by foreclosures or unable to buy, America's residential rental market is alive and doing well. More than 3 million people have been added to the renter pool, rents have jumped 20 percent since the bubble and are predicted to increase 3.5 percent nationwide this year, and the vacancy rate is down to about 5 percent (and even less in some areas).

Single-family rental investing is a $3 trillion market, although in terms of capitalization rates or "cap rates," certain markets are much more attractive than others when it comes to profitability of an investment home. (Cap rates are essentially the return on your investment; you measure the profitability of an investment property by taking the expense-adjusted annual cash flow from renting a property relative to the acquisition price.)

If you've never invested in residential rental properties before, here are a few of the factors you may want to consider:

- *Neighborhood.* Stable, low-crime, moderate-income neighborhoods that are within close proximity to large employers, military bases, schools, shopping centers, and healthcare facilities tend to be reliable investments. Lower-end properties tend to have higher returns but more headaches. Twenty minutes or less is an ideal distance from your own home, as this is convenient and allows you to appear involved and available to your tenants.

- *Property Type.* Single-family properties provide the easiest way to get into real estate investing and build equity fast during times of rising prices. If you own multiple homes, it can be a lot of work to collect rent and maintain them vs. an apartment building with a similar number of units.

Small multiple-unit residential rental properties, including duplexes, triplexes, and fourplexes, are often a good compromise.

- *Size, Design, and Amenities.* Tenants may like what you like. And curb appeal counts. But also look from a maintenance standpoint for simplicity: ease of access to ductwork, heating pipes, plumbing, and electric lines buried in or beneath the slab. Look for simple construction and simple landscaping. Consider hurricanes, flooding, and other mischief caused by Mother Nature, depending on where you're located.

- *Condition.* Depending on how handy you are, a professional inspector may be appropriate. Radon, lead paint, asbestos, and mold are four primary concerns. Plan to do upgrades to justify rent increases.

- *Financial.* In real estate, the money is made when you buy, so you must buy right. Think about your exit before you get in. Eventually you will want to sell. Does the property and price lend itself to appreciating? In the meantime, you'll need to generate enough income from the rental property to cover the expenses and throw off a profit. Know what your costs will be and what rent you can charge.

- *Management.* Screening tenants and managing repairs are essential to making rental property the best possible investment. You'll also need to know landlord-tenant laws. It is advisable to consult a lawyer to ensure that your other assets will be protected in the event of a lawsuit. For more on this subject, check out the online video clips at www.askshario.com/buyingforeclosures and www.askshario.com/reoforeclosures.

Many investors today are specifically targeting distressed rental properties and there's plenty of opportunity in all price ranges, property types, and areas. There are several important differences between buying a distressed property and buying a property under more normal circumstances. For example:

- *Cooperation.* Listing agents, asset managers, and decision makers at banks don't have the same incentives as a regular home seller. They're all handling a lot of deals, not just one. And their primary concern is CYA and their paycheck.

- *History.* No one can provide background for you like a seller who actually lived in the home.

- *Inspections and Repairs.* Properties may be in poor condition, and you may have limited access for inspections.

- *Contract and Negotiation.* You'll have to use bank form contracts and disclosures and have little leverage.

- *Financing.* Your money typically needs to be lined up in advance.

- *Title.* You need to be extra careful with a foreclosure that the title work was done properly and there are no other liens.

- *Possession.* You may need to evict the owner or tenant.

Fortunately, there are certain actions you can take to mitigate these risks. First and foremost is choosing the right professional, someone who knows the neighborhood and has experience working with distressed properties and banks. Second, you need to do your own homework as well. Research the neighborhood. Once you find a property, check out its history in the public records. Talk to neighbors, too. You'll be surprised how much they will be able share.

Last, but certainly not least, you'll need to prepare in advance for opportunity. Line up your financing (particularly if you live in a market where you'll compete against investors, you need to be able to act fast like a cash investor); also line up your inspectors, lawyer and closing company, and appraiser. In terms of financing, and especially if the property you're buying needs work, the FHA 203(k) loan, explained in the sidebar, may be worth considering for inclusion in your financial fresh start. Also read and get comfortable with the contracts and disclosures you'll have to sign. And be persistent! If your offer is rejected, wait thirty days and submit again. Unfortunately, there are plenty of homes to go around. If you put in the time and elbow grease, it will definitely pay off.

One-Minute Mentor:
What Is the FHA 203(K) Loan?

It is not uncommon for folks trying to buy a home today to find that many of the homes they see are in poor shape because of the prior owner's financial challenges. Homes whose sellers are short-selling or homes that have been foreclosed are in notoriously poor shape. If you're like most folks, you don't have enough cash to cover a down payment, closing costs, *and* renovation expenses for a house. The 203(k) is a little-known FHA loan available to almost anyone who wants to buy a home that needs work or even refinance and renovate their own home. It's the perfect solution if you want to make money on foreclosures but don't have enough cash for the down payment, closing costs, and renovation costs.

For more information on the FHA 203(k), see online video at **www.askshario.com/fhaloan.**

What About Fresh Start Opportunities Investing in Commercial Real Estate?

Commercial real estate encompasses several different types of properties including office, retail, hotel, industrial, and larger multifamily buildings. Other than the fact that you will likely need to come up with a larger down payment if you plan to finance your purchases, investing in small commercial real estate is actually no more difficult than investing in residential rental properties (in fact, in some ways, managing commercial real estate is even easier than managing residential), but the risks can vary. This is because most commercial real estate tenants are businesses, not individuals and families. The dynamics are not the same as they are when your tenant needs a roof over her head. If the business doesn't do well, your rental income is at risk. In addition to price and rent per square foot, the primary indicators in commercial real estate are vacancy and absorption rates.

So what's going on in commercial real estate in the new economy? The sidebar provides you with a quick recap based on current predictions by the experts, which are, of course, always in flux.

As with residential real estate, commercial real estate is location sensitive. As you can imagine, the demand for office, industrial, retail, and even hotel properties depends a lot on the local and broader economy and employment levels, as well as on the amount of new construction in each of these categories, all factors to consider if commercial real estate investing is part of your fresh start plan.

For more information, see the video clip at www.askshario.com/smallbizrealestate.

A Quick Commercial Real Estate Snapshot

- **Office Space.** According to some experts, vacancy rates are in the 16 percent range but expected to drop. Rents are up and expected to rise further, but by only 2 percent to 3 percent over the next few years.

- **Industrial.** Vacancy rates are in the 12 percent range but expected to drop. Rents are up and expected to rise further, but only 2 percent to 5 percent over the next few years.

- **Retail.** Vacancy rates are in the 13 percent range. Rents are up and expected to rise further, but by only one percent to 3 percent.

- **Multifamily Units.** Vacancy rates are notably low, at under 5 percent (anything under 5 percent is considered a "landlord's market"). Rents have been rising and are expected to continue rising 4 percent to 6 percent over the next few years. Up-to-the-minute indicators of this nature are easily available for commercial real estate from a multitude of sources.

The Bottom Line

It wasn't long ago that the homeownership vs. renting debate was a no-brainer. But in the new economy that's not the case for everybody anymore. Some folks today are questioning whether homeownership is right for them or even a solid place to invest their hard-earned money. The new short-term triage rules and reforms are intended to help keep folks in their homes. But it's undeniable that the new longer-term rules and reforms, and certainly the new economy dynamics surrounding homeownership in general, risk changing the role that homeownership has historically played for Americans—perhaps forever. There are potentially far-reaching implications for America's middle class (who have historically relied more heavily on home equity for their personal wealth than other demographics have), but also for everybody else who, as shareholders in The America Company, may very well wind up paying the price for the shortfall if the important role home equity plays is allowed to become a void.

After all is said and done, 84 percent of Americans still consider real estate a good long-term investment. If you decide to include homeownership in your own savings, investing, and retirement fresh start plan, then striving to own your home free and clear is the way to go. And keeping any eye out for ongoing new rules and reforms from Washington that impact your homeownership is a wise way to make sure your most valuable investment remains safe. The next chapter, which details the final step in your financial fresh start, shows you how to spend less and earn more under the new economy rules and reforms. Who among us can't use a little bit of that nowadays!

CHAPTER SIX

Step Five:
Spend Less and Earn More

- **What Will You Learn from This Chapter?** This chapter will teach you how to use the knowledge you have to balance your budget by spending even less, but also by earning more.

- **How Will This Know-How Help You?** Balancing your budget is the first step toward achieving a sense of balance in the rest of your life and well-being! Success is comfortably living within your financial means, more easily setting aside savings and investment money, and confidently ensuring your fresh start prosperity for the years ahead.

Let's face it, if you're like most folks in the new economy, your fresh start plan is simply going to have to include some strategies for spending less, earning more, or some combination of the two. We begin with spending less because it tends to be where you can start making changes right away. (If you know you overspend, then also revisit Chapter 3, for some strategies to figure out the emotional reasons behind why you buy.)

Spending Less

If you feel you've gotten pretty good at not wasting money on nonessentials, you may be surprised to find that even the list of *essentials* in most American households has extended to way beyond what it was when most of us were kids. Take electronics and technology, for example. The monthly service fees on your "essential" electronics and technology alone probably add up to more money than your parents spent each month for real "life-or-death" essentials, such as groceries. Your smartphone (along with all of those add-on fees for multimedia, e-mail, and texting), cable television, Sirius radio, Internet access, iPads, Nooks, Kindles, and all of that electronic downloading you do on iTunes, Netflix, Amazon, and who knows where else with a single click, sure can add up! Especially if you've got a spouse and kids doing the same thing. And what about clothing? It was not long ago that every kid wore Lee or Levi's® jeans and donned a pair of canvas Chuck Taylors or Keds PF Flyers on their feet. It's not uncommon for today's American family, on the other hand, to spend more on a single pair of the latest Nikes or designer jeans than an entire back-to-school wardrobe cost when most of us were that age! Thanks to America's middle class and the collective reach for upward mobility and success (or at least the appearance of it), not to mention Madison Avenue, you'd need earplugs and a lobotomy to insulate yourself from all of the spending opportunities that pummel you at every turn. Hundreds of billions of dollars are spent each year by some of the smartest advertisers in the world, all to get you to spend your money on whatever it is that they're hawking. Mind you, these are not your father's clear, straightforward advertising campaigns, either. These folks know more about how to influence you (without you even realizing you're being influenced) than you can ever imagine. If your fresh start plan does not include measurable, accessible, easy-to-stick-with strategies for spending less, these guys will easily outsmart you and succeed in separating you from your hard-earned money every time!

Unfortunately, there are no new rules and reforms aimed at protecting you from this particular "financial hazard." The new Consumer Financial Protection Bureau can't protect you from the consequences of your own spending. This part's up to you.

Since you're reading this book, you've probably already gone through your budget and axed the bigger expenses that jumped out at you. If you have not yet done that, check out the easy worksheet I've included for you in the online Appendix.

Most folks find that a handful of their biggest expenses together add up to almost two-thirds of their entire expenditures. Spending less on these "biggies" is thus typically the first line of defense in your spending fresh start attack. While everybody's expenses vary, this chapter begins with examples of two "biggie" expenses that impact many folks: real estate tax and insurance.

Getting a Fresh Start on Your Biggie Real Estate Tax Expense

With so many folks in desperate need of ways to reduce their monthly housing costs, it's great to know that there are ways to do that without having to count on your bank to help you out with a modification. Reducing your real estate taxes can potentially save you thousands of dollars each year. Banks are doing just that on a large scale with all the foreclosures they now own. By taking a few simple steps you can get the same benefits! Property tax petition services are also available to handle this process for you if you prefer, typically charging 20 percent to 30 percent of the tax that they save you in the first year.

Taxes, of course, are government's "allowance." It's how the public services that help run and support everybody are paid for. States grant taxing authority (usually in state statutes) to various entities, such as local municipalities, water and sewer districts, and school boards, for various purposes. Each state establishes its own framework in its statutes for deciding how much folks will pay for real estate taxes. In Florida, for example, the Florida Department of Revenue has the "Uniform Policies and Procedures Manual," decided by statute, that governs each county. Each county itself establishes the exact procedures it will follow within the confines of Florida's statutory framework. County property appraisers are in charge of establishing the value for each property in their counties as of a set time each year. The county tax collector then calculates the real estate taxes for your home and sends you a notice.

So how can you save money on your real estate taxes? First, consider how your taxes were calculated. Ask the property appraiser's office to explain how property values are determined in your area. For example, it may use the purchase price you paid and then revisit recent sales by area every few years to adjust for market changes. Other property appraisers use replacement cost. Your local property appraiser's website should have this information ready and waiting for you. Once you understand how the base value of a home is calculated, become familiar with the features that add or deduct value to or from your home—including square footage, the age of the home, lot size, and so on—so that you will be able to compare your property and the value it's been given for tax purposes to other properties and the values they've been assigned.

Next, do your research on sales of similar homes in your area with an eye toward understanding why your home may be valued higher or lower. You can find this information in tax records or by asking a Realtor friend. If your property taxes seem high for your neighborhood and there's a lot of money at stake, some folks engage an independent appraiser to help (usually for a few hundred dollars). What you're trying to show is that your property is valued by the county for more than it should be, based on how other properties have been valued. What you paid for your property is one piece of proof, but the real issue is what your home is worth now, which is usually, but not always, about what you paid.

Summarize the evidence you've found in writing. Note that your financial circumstance is not relevant to this process. Folks sometimes confuse this process with asking for a mortgage modification. The bank does care if you can afford to pay your mortgage. The real estate tax and adjustment board will not consider whether you can afford to pay your taxes, and referencing your personal financial circumstances may impact your credibility.

If, as with many folks, your property value has gone down and the value being used to calculate your property taxes is, therefore, too high, your state statutes generally give you the legal right to contest the tax amount (see One-Minute Mentor: Contesting Your Property Taxes).

Check out this helpful video clip (www.askshario.com/lowertaxes) and the online Appendix for more information about how you can, depending on your state, fresh start your real estate tax expenses by reducing them.

If you have a mortgage and escrow payments with your bank for your real estate taxes, don't forget to make sure that your lender is notified that your real estate taxes have been reduced. It may take some time for your bank to adjust the real estate tax escrow portion of your mortgage loan payment and any refunds that you're due from your escrow account.

One-Minute Mentor:
Contesting Your Property Taxes

The exact procedure for legally contesting the property value assigned to your home varies by state. The following is an example of the procedure in Florida:

1. *Meeting.* Request an individual meeting with the Property Appraiser's office.

2. *Hearing.* If you are not satisfied with the outcome of that meeting, you have the legal right to contest the Property Appraiser's valuation of your home by filing a "Petition to the Value Adjustment Board— Request for Hearing." The Value Adjustment Board will then listen to your evidence and decide whether your property taxes should be lowered.

3. *Lawsuit.* If you disagree with the Value Adjustment Board's decision, you have the legal right to file a lawsuit. In Florida, the applicable laws are FS 194.011 (5) (b) and Fla Admin Code 12 D-9 and 10 and 16.002.

Getting a Fresh Start on Your Biggie Insurance Expenses

Even though the types of insurance that got AIG involved in the bailout were more complicated insurance products, AIG is oftentimes credited with putting the insurance industry on the radar screen for new rules and reforms. You know that one of the main goals of the new rules and reforms is to protect you from risky financial products and services. Insurance products and services are already regulated by each state. Accordingly, insurance products and services are largely excluded from the new Consumer Financial Protection Bureau's authority. In fact, Dodd-Frank specifically makes it clear that insurance companies, and even insurance company bailouts, will continue to be resolved under state law. (The Federal Deposit Insurance Corporation can step in to wind down a systemically important insurance company only if the state insurance commissioner for the state in which the insurance company is located does not do so.)

Dodd-Frank does establish the Federal Insurance Office with information-gathering powers, but other than that, the insurance industry emerged relatively unchanged. Before the Federal Insurance Office can even collect any data from insurers, it first needs to "coordinate with each relevant federal agency and state insurance regulator … and any publicly available sources to determine if the information to be collected is available from, and may be obtained in a timely manner by, such federal agency or state insurance regulator … or publicly available source." The Federal Insurance Office is also now in charge of conducting a study and submitting a report to Congress on how to modernize and improve the system of insurance regulation and minority and low- and moderate-income access to affordable insurance products. That could be good news for folks who have not been able to get insurance coverage. On the other hand, some experts believe that introducing uniformity to a marketplace accustomed to local supervision could have unintended consequences, including decreasing competition. Dodd-Frank also left some issues, particularly involving life insurance, to be addressed by thirteen different federal agencies through more than 150 separate new rule-making and reform directives. That's a heck of a lot of issues to resolve within an unclear timeline; so if one of your own spending fresh start biggies is life insurance, keep an eye out. The cost and coverage of your life insurance may be impacted by the new rules and reforms.

In the meantime, other spending biggies for most folks include home, health, life, car, and disability insurance, which, for some people, can add up to tens of thousands of dollars a year. All of these types of insurance provide potential areas in which you may be able to spend less.

On the other hand, insurance is a spending biggie that tends to get pushed to the back burner. For some folks, cutting insurance spending just seems complicated and time-consuming. Others worry more about not being able to get coverage in the first place and just take what they can get without asking. There are numerous fresh start strategies for spending less on your homeowner's insurance, as described in the next sections; spending less for your other insurance products can be approached in much the same way.

Fresh Start Tips for Your Biggie Expenses—Insurance

As long as you have coverage, folks don't pay too much attention to insurance. But insurance, especially homeowner's insurance and especially in some parts of the country such as the Southeast and California (which happen to also be among the hardest hit states), is a huge cost for a lot of folks. And in many cases it's one that can be easily lowered if you do a little legwork now and make a habit of checking back again each year before your insurance renews.

The low-lying fruit, when it comes to saving money on insurance, is raising your deductible. It is the single easiest way to lower insurance costs. Insurance is not supposed to be for smaller mishaps. If you use it that way, over time your premiums will go through the roof. Raising your deductible, for example, from $500 to $1,000, can save as much as 25 percent on your annual premium! If you put that annual savings away, it will add up to more than enough to cover the higher deductible should you ever need it.

Here are some other fresh start tips related to homeowner's insurance:

- *Look into buying your home, car, and other insurance from the same company.* Some companies offer "multiline" discounts if you do so.

- *Ask about home improvements that will reduce your premium.* Some companies offer discounts if you add dead bolt locks, window locks, or an alarm system, for example. Discounts are also available sometimes if you upgrade to newer electric, heating, or plumbing systems. All of these, in theory, reduce the chance that you will have a claim from, for example, a burglary or fire.

- *Make sure you're not paying for unneeded coverage.* For most folks, there are several areas in which this advice may apply. For example, you may have coverage for additional items such as fancy electronics that are no longer worth as much. Or your coverage may be based on the value of your property when you bought it, when it is now worth less. Also, you should never buy insurance coverage for the land since dirt is not at risk for perils. On another note, often insurance premiums are now tied to your credit score. If your score has gone up, ask about having your premiums lowered.

Shop around and be sure you're comparing apples to apples. Most folks would never consider spending thousands of dollars on a new video camera, for example, without first doing their homework to ensure they are getting the features they want, not paying for features they don't want, and getting the best price they can find. Yet many people don't bother to put the same effort into spending the same amount every year, year after year, on insurance. As with any other major purchase, especially one you make over and over again, it pays to shop around and compare. Ask your friends or check with your state's insurance department or the National Association of Insurance Commissioners (www.naic.org). You'll also find great fresh start tips for finding the very best insurance agent in Chapter 7.

One more tip if you're thinking about buying a new home or investment property: Be sure to ask for the Comprehensive Loss Underwriting Exchange (CLUE) report for the home. It will give you an idea of how much you will be paying for insurance, which in regions where insurance premiums are high can cost you even more than a mortgage. (And even when your mortgage is paid off, you'll still be needing insurance!)

Some interesting new insurance challenges have arisen thanks to the real estate and foreclosure crises. Folks facing foreclosure tend not to be thinking about what their insurance policy says will happen to their coverage if their home goes into foreclosure, becomes vacant, or is rented out. Folks having to relocate for work or move into a nursing home without first being able to sell their home (due to today's real estate market constraints) may face insurance policy issues. Similar insurance hiccups arise with more frequency nowadays as sellers remain in the home after selling it or deeding it back to their bank or as buyers ask to move into vacant homes before closing. For more on insurance dos and don'ts such as these, including other ways to save on your homeowners, car, health, life, and disability insurance, check out the online Appendix and the video clip at www.askshario. com/insurance.

Looking Beyond the Biggies

Truthfully, even once you've axed the two biggie spending numbers— real estate tax and insurance expenses—there's still always room for more. It's just that round two of your spending cuts is going to come in a lot of little pieces from a lot of different places. But those little numbers add up, and you'll be amazed to learn how many new ways you can continually find to spend less once you make doing so a top-of-mind priority. For example, average Americans spend more than 12 percent on food and between 5 and 10 percent of their annual budget on fuel. The video clip at www.askshario.com/saveatthepump explains fresh start ways to save at the pump. And you'll find plenty of other wonderful resources to help spot all the little ways to easily cut spending every day under "Ways to Save" in the online Appendix. It's also a good idea to revisit your fresh start budget at least once each year and anytime there's a big change in your income or expenses.

Loyalty and Reward Programs: Do They Help You Save or Cost You More?

On the hand other, as you are cutting back, be aware of the gimmicks that some businesses use to trick you into spending *more* by thinking that you're being frugal and spending less. (The subject of loyalty and reward programs was briefly referenced in the context of credit cards in Chapter 2; now let's discuss it in more detail.) For example, the larger retail stores and credit card companies sometimes use loyalty and rewards programs to entice you to spend more by promising to save you money. You've no doubt seen the offers: a percentage off of your purchase when you apply for a card, free shipping if you register, a percentage off of purchases if you join the program, and other special offers and discounts for "members." Many of these offers sound wonderful. But does trying to save money this way really pay off, or can being frugal cost you big bucks?

Today, 86 percent of Americans buy into these offers, literally and figuratively. And they can indeed be a wonderful way to spend less *if* you know the secrets—how to use these programs to your benefit.

But if you don't, you're likely to wind up spending even more, which is exactly why the companies making you these offers make them in the first place. After all, they're not in business to lose money! Loyalty or rewards programs are expensive for companies to run. One thing that you can be sure of is that, especially in the new economy, the companies offering these programs are earning back every penny they spend on these programs and then some. The sidebar opposite explains the skinny on some of the ways they do just that.

Fresh Start Tips for Loyalty and Reward Programs

The good news is there are steps that you can take to ensure that your own personal fresh start takes full advantages of the opportunities that loyalty, rewards, and other incentives programs provide while avoiding the pitfalls. Here are a few of those steps.

First, before signing up for one of these programs, look at your current lifestyle and spending and sign up only for programs that you are certain will pay off, based on things you already need and buy and amounts you're already spending. When you're offered these incentives at the cash register, don't sign up on the spot. That's what retailers are counting on! Instead, ask to take the application or other information home so that you can read it carefully and think about signing up the next time that you're in the store.

Plan ahead for big expenses. For example, if you will be renovating your home, check out a Home Depot, Lowe's, or other home improvement retailer's loyalty or reward program.

And, as always, read the fine print. Pay special attention to the annual percentage rate (APR), annual fees, grace periods, over-the-limit fees, late fees, when default APR kicks in, the amount of time

One-Minute Mentor:
The Inside Skinny on Loyalty and Rewards Programs

Many times the profit that companies generate from a loyalty and reward program lies in the "fine print" terms of the program itself. For example, companies may make a profit by:

- Requiring minimum purchase amounts, so you will spend more than you would have otherwise spent if you did not sign up for the loyalty or reward program

- Offering a discount "on your next purchase" so that you will come back and spend again when you otherwise would not have

- Making you mail in a rebate form in order to earn the discount you were promised (when companies know most folks will not take the time and remember to mail in rebates)

- Limiting the items or purchases to which the rewards apply

- Qualifying that your rewards are forfeited or expire after a certain amount of time

- Sometimes charging you higher interest or other fees

These programs also often track the brands, frequencies, or amounts of purchases you make and then send you very targeted customized advertisements (which translates to advertisements that are even harder for you to resist) in order to get you to spend more money than you otherwise would have. Sometimes the programs themselves are outsourced to third-party vendors, who can then use your information to send you targeted advertisements from other affiliates, again resulting in you spending more, not less!

default APR can last, when the interest can change, and limitations on rewards.

Many of these programs require an e-mail address to register. Set up an e-mail account just for these solicitations; that way you can know when you are getting an e-mail designed to get you to spend more that can be traced to a program that was supposed to save you money. Then use that delete button frequently!

Check out the video clip at www.askshario.com/frugal.

Earning More in the New Economy

America was built on individualism, hard work, ingenuity, and good old-fashioned capitalism ... essentially the drive to earn more. That's exactly what the new economy calls for! When it comes to earning more in the new economy, most folks fall into one of three categories: those who *have to* earn more, those who *would like to* earn more (including folks who are fine with their current level of earning but have some concern over job security), and those who are happy with their earning level. This section covers fresh start tips for the first two categories. If you're lucky enough to be in the third category, feel free to skip right over this section!

The fact that there are a limited number of big-picture approaches to earning more money is, at once, both a blessing and a curse. It's a blessing because a limited number of possibilities makes it easier for you to decide, relatively quickly, which approach or approaches work best for you. It's a curse, of course, because you simply have to make one or more of these approaches work for you. If you're not nuts about any of them, too bad. Unless your plan is to win the lottery or inherit millions from a rich relative (in which case you may want to line up a plan B, just in case), loosely speaking your big-picture approach to earning more money has to incorporate one or more of the following:

- Earning more from your current job(s)

- Changing your current job(s) entirely to one or more alternative job(s) that will enable you to earn more

- Adding one or more additional part-time job(s) or revenue sources to your plan

Chapter 8 will help you to solidify your longer-term fresh start plan for prosperity, including enhancing your qualifications to increase your income at your current job(s) and changing your current job(s) and career entirely. This chapter's material focuses instead on shorter-term fresh start strategies for additional job(s) and revenue sources. You can implement these strategies in your own personal fresh start plan relatively quickly and starting right away.

The quickest fresh start strategies for earning more fall into three basic buckets: 1) converting your assets to cash; 2) investing your own time to generate income; or 3) investing your own resources to create a business where other folks' time (along with your own time) will generate cash profit for you. So, basically, we're talking about selling your stuff, getting a part-time job, or starting a side business.

Clearly, selling some of your things for cash has limitations in that each sale generates a onetime blast of cash and then it's done. Some tips for this quick but somewhat limited approach to earning more in the immediate future are covered for you in the online Appendix. The remaining buckets—investing your own time and/or resources to generate income—are covered in more detail for you in the next few sections.

Part-Time Jobs in the New Economy

Getting one or more part-time jobs is clearly a more sustainable approach to earning more. While everyone's circumstances, skill set, and ideal part-time job are different, here is some general advice if you'd like to make a part-time job a component of your fresh start plan for earning more.

To ensure that you're happy with the fresh start part-time job you find, before you even begin looking, consider a few important things, such as the number of hours and time of day you want to work and how flexible the job needs to be. Do you want to work from home or on location? How much do you want to earn? Do you want to work for someone else or create your own second job? Do you want to think about different jobs for different times of the year?

Getting a second job to earn more money does not have to be all work and no fun. As is the case with every challenge you face in life, you and you alone choose how you wish to view it, and this choice oftentimes separates folks who succeed in life and happiness from those who do not. Maybe you want to think a bit outside of the box when it comes to a second job and do something different (how about letting a company actually pay you to wrap the car you drive in an advertisement!). Maybe this is an opportunity for adventure, perhaps exploring an interest or even a career change that you've been considering.

Once you're clear on the "non-negotiables," it's time to prepare yourself to put your best foot forward. A simple résumé and references are in order. Unless you've been given other instructions, business casual attire is appropriate for most part-time or second job in-person interviews. Even if you're not one to fuss, taking a little extra time on grooming your hair and nails (and makeup for the ladies) can be well worth the investment. Being on time for your appointment is a must.

Be conscious of your body language, eye contact, and posture—it all translates into the image you want to convey as a candid and confident employee. Plenty has been written about résumé writing and interview skills if you feel outside of your comfort zone and need to brush up on these areas.

Thanks to the Internet, this is not your father's job search. Online resources for part-time and second jobs abound, along with less formal venues, such as Craigslist. You can browse for positions that look interesting from the comfort of your own cozy couch and even post your own skill set and interests for employers to find you. Asking friends, family, and neighbors for job leads is another surefire way to know you're connecting with qualified employers, and both you and your prospective employer get the added comfort of knowing that the person who introduced you would not have done so if she didn't think it might be a good fit.

Some jobs just naturally lend themselves to part-timers, meaning you may find that there are more of these types of jobs available. Among the top 10 part-time job areas you may want to consider are:

- *Computer-Related Jobs:* data entry, tech support, and programming if you have those skills

- *Secretarial:* answering service, appointment scheduling, transcribing (medical and other), customer service, call centers, virtual assistant

- *Accounting:* billing (medical and other), auditing, collections

- *Sales:* telemarketing, retail (e.g., cashier, sales clerk), PR, publicity, and marketing

- *Teaching:* academic subjects, job skills training, sport and fitness training, career or life coaching

- *Caregiving:* child, elder, or pet care

- *Food and Beverage:* waitress, bartender, caterer, baker, pizza delivery, valet parking

- *Writing and Artistic:* writing assignments, graphic design (e.g., logos, web), photography, decorating, if you have those skills

- *Handyman (or woman):* lawns, landscaping, snow removal, cleaning or janitorial work, repairs' and maintenance (e.g., home, car, boat), carpentry

- *Transporting:* trash removal, moving services, drivers (transporting goods or people)

In the event that you're not a good fit for a particular job or employer, prepare yourself for "no," but always keep the door open. You never know when employers' needs may change. With part-time and second jobs, you'll need to be especially careful not to overcommit and potentially impact your primary job. You may need to be more patient than you might otherwise like and wait until you find the right fit.

Unfortunately, as seems to be commonplace in all areas of life where the scammers know people may be desperate, be aware of the bad guys. For example, once you dig into your job search, you are bound to see advertisements for part-time work that you can do in your own home. While some of these offers are legitimate, they also rank among the most common scams. They may include offers to pay you for stuffing envelopes, assembling things, or "helping" you start your own home business. The red flag is that they will almost always ask you to buy materials up-front or pay some other sort of up-front fee. These scammers are out looking for more vulnerable stay-at-home moms or low-income, less educated, elderly, or disabled folks who will take their bait. The moral of this story is that, as the age-old golden rule reminds you, if it sounds too good to be true, it probably is. Some good rules of thumb are to (1) always verify that you're dealing with a real (credible) established company, (2) never respond to blind ads, (3) ask to speak with someone in human resources, and (4) verify that there is a real job description. Employers who don't even bother to take the time to qualify you through some sort of process are more likely to be sketchy.

If you've always been one to spend as much money as you've earned, that's a habit you'll absolutely want to correct, otherwise you'll be undermining your fresh start plan. The main reason for getting a second or part-time job is to balance your budget and secure your prosperous financial future, so you'll want to be sure you actually set aside the income you earn from your new job as planned. And, if your employer is not going to be paying your income taxes, while you're at it, don't forget to set enough aside to pay your income taxes.

Happy job hunting!

(For more information, check out the video clip at www. askshario.com/earnmore.)

Direct Sales 101

Another approach to earning more in the new economy is direct sales. This is an area that actually combines some of the benefits of a part-time job working for other folks with a part-time business you own yourself. In a nutshell, direct selling is marketing and selling products or services directly to consumers, away from the traditional fixed retail location. You may have heard of companies such as Mary Kay or Avon. Direct sales is the oldest form of sales. The direct sales business has grown by almost 80 percent in the last few years, and there are now thousands of direct sale companies in hundreds of different industries selling everything from jewelry to scrapbooking supplies to clothing to pet products. The sidebar lists examples of direct sales opportunities by category and industry.

Some folks are skeptical of the direct sales model, and direct sales is not for everyone (for reasons that I'll mention shortly). If you need to increase your income, however, it is definitely worth considering direct sales as an earnings opportunity. Direct selling is now a $117 billion worldwide industry, with $28.56 billion of those sales occurring right here in America. More than 60 million folks worldwide and 15.8 million Americans are earning more through direct sales. On the other side of the equation, more than half of America's adult population has purchased goods or some form of services, at some point, through a direct sales channel. That's about 150 million people. So we're talking about a huge market with lots of opportunity and alternatives.

Among the advantages of direct sales are flexibility, low cost to get started, ability to work from home, ability to make your own hours and do as much sales (or as little) as you want, social interaction with like-minded people, a chance to develop new skills, and the fact that literally anyone can try it. On the other hand, there are pitfalls: You really do need to be self-disciplined and have a general idea about business planning. You must be sure you find the right product or service and a good company fit (you may need to try out a few different products or companies before you find the right one). And again, you must beware the scammers.

If you want to include direct sales in your fresh start plan for earning more money, first off, get clear about your financial goals. That includes both your long- and short-term goals (for example, you may want to earn more money in order to pay for a new car),

Direct Sales: Product and Service Categories and Industries

Air Filters/Air Filtration Systems

Animal/Pet Care

Aromatherapy

Art/Framing

Audio/CDs/Cassettes

Autocare

Baby/Childcare

Baskets

Bed and Bath

Benefits Packages

Books

Brokerage Services

Business/Commercial

Candles/Candle Accessories

Clothing/Shoes

Coffee/Tea/Specialty Beverages

Cookware

Cosmetics

Crafts/Craft Supplies

Crystal/China

Cutlery

Educational Materials

Encyclopedias

Fashion Accessories

Financial Services

Food/Gourmet Items

Fragrances

Garden Accessories

Giftware

Green/Organic/Eco-Friendly Products

Group Buying Services

Haircare/Hair Accessories

Health/Fitness/Wellness

Holiday Decorations

Home Accessories/Décor

Home Appliances

Home Technology

Homecare

Homeopathics

Housewares/Kitchenwares

Insurance

Internet Services

Jewelry

Legal Services

Lingerie/Sleepwear

Nutritional Supplements

Oral Hygiene

Party Supplies

Personal Care

Photography/Photo Processing

Plants/Foliage

Real Estate Services

Religious Books/Gifts

Rubber Stamps

Scrapbooking/Photo Albums

Security Systems/Devices

Skincare

Software/Computers

Spa Products

Sporting Goods

Stationery/Paper Products

Tableware

Telecommunications Services

Tools

Toys/Games

Travel

Utilities

Vacuum Cleaners

Videos

Water Treatment Systems

Weight Management

Wine/Wine Accessories

Note: Specific companies mentioned in this chapter's discussion of direct sales are for purposes of example only and should not be considered endorsements.

how much you want to earn, and how much time you can spend on the job.

Second, assess your comfort level. What company, product, or service do you find appealing or perhaps already use and like? If possible, attend an event for the direct sale company you are considering in order to get a better feel for how the company operates.

Third, do your homework. Before you accept a job doing direct sales, find out all you can about:

- *The Company:* Check out the company website as well as blogs, the Better Business Bureau, and consumer protection agencies. Are there any complaints against the company? Inquire of folks you know who already work for the company or in its industry. Does the company have a proven track record? (For example, Avon has 6.5 million worldwide reps and annual sales over $8 billion.) Is the company a member of the Direct Selling Association (one of the industry's main trade associations)?

- *The Products:* Does the company sell quality products or services? Is there a need for these goods and services? Are they competitively priced? (Retailers spend up to 25 percent to 30 percent on advertising, warehousing, and shipping while direct sales companies eliminate these middlemen and should price their offerings accordingly.) Does the company stand behind its products and services? Do you feel comfortable selling them? Most important, do you really believe in the company and its products?

- *The Start-Up Costs:* Direct sales start-up costs are generally modest. Most companies offer a starter kit (for example, Arbonne, the skincare company, sells a $29 preferred client starter kit or a $79 consultant starter kit). Often these starter kits cost under $100 because direct sales companies want to make it easy for you to get started.

- *The Tools and Training:* Will you be instructed on how to run the business? Product knowledge? Does the company have an opportunity for ongoing skills building? For example, Arbonne provides a product catalog, company brochure, success plan, and policies and procedure manual. And most of the larger direct sales companies have regularly scheduled sales and training events. Some even have mentor programs.

- *The Income:* How is your compensation going to be structured? How much money do you anticipate you will earn? Does the company offer recognitions and incentives? Do they help motivate you? For example, Arbonne motivates its direct sales folks by providing achievement levels, including a preferred client level, consultant level, district manager level, executive district manager level, area manager level, executive area manager level, regional vice president level, and for the top salespeople, an executive regional vice president level. Each level up includes more incentives. Companies such as Arbonne and Mary Kay also offer product discounts, bonuses, overrides, cars, trips, jewelry, and other rewards for top sellers.

- *The Laws:* Are there federal and state laws you need to know about, including laws addressing earnings, product claims, and other potential issues? For example, each state has a three-day cooling off period to allow consumers to reconsider direct sales contracts. The Securities and Exchange Commission (SEC) and U.S. Postal Service have anti–pyramid scheme laws. In addition, you will likely be considered an independent contractor, and most direct sales companies require you to sign some kind of agreement. A 1099 form must be filed if you are paid more than $600 or purchase more than $5,000 worth of products from the company.

One-Minute Mentor: Recruiting Is Not Selling

A direct sale company's income should be based solely on your sales. Stay away if you're told that you get paid primarily by using products yourself or by recruiting new folks. Recruiting others should be optional if you wish to expand business this way or help train others. It should not be required or the only way that you can achieve your income goals. Your compensation must always be based on actual sales to actual customers. Make sure the stated goal is to sell to end users, not to new recruits. Never buy more inventory yourself than you are confident you can sell. Legitimate companies make money as you sell and make money, too. In fact, 34 percent of direct sellers do not even include recruiting in their business.

Finally, it bears repeating: Be aware of the scammers. They try to make money off of *you*. The shady guys tend to make their money from fees paid by new recruits, and they demand that you load up on inventory or training aids, for example. High start-up entry fees are a red flag. Also, be on the lookout for companies that encourage you to buy a lot in order to reach discount levels or achieve certain sale levels. What are the terms for returns? Members of the Direct Selling Association are required to buy back your unsold inventory for at least 90 percent of what you paid for them if you quit within twelve months.

If you're considering direct sales as a way to earn more for your fresh start strategy, it may help you to know that most folks who try direct selling say they make more than enough money during the first year to cover the costs. A surprising 84 percent say they make more money than they expected. And 78 percent say they will continue as a direct seller in the future. The turnover in direct sales is comparable to turnover in traditional employment, but many folks drop out only to step in again later, when they have a new financial short-term goal. If you're interested in direct sales, check out the video clip at www.askshario.com/directsales.

Are Franchise Businesses for You?

Maybe your fresh start plan includes earning more, but getting a part-time job or direct sales are not for you. Maybe you've always dreamed of owning your own business but are not sure exactly how to go about it or are concerned about the costs and risks. This may be your big fresh start opportunity!

The Pros and Cons of Franchising

Small businesses are the backbone of the American economy. If you're thinking about starting one and are comfortable doing so, good for you! But if you are like other folks, who feel they will benefit from more guidance and structure when it comes to opening a business, you may find your comfort level in opening a franchise. In fact, franchising accounts for about 50 percent of all retail sales in the United States, already employs over 15 million Americans, and creates almost $2 trillion in revenue every year worldwide. With franchises, you generally buy the right to operate the business for a certain amount of time (typically five to thirty-five years with renewals) and within a certain territory.

The franchise concept can be traced all the way back to rickshaw routes in China as early as 200 BC. Here in America, the Singer Sewing Machine Company couldn't afford salaried salesmen and began using the franchise model back in the 1850s. General Motors and Ford couldn't afford bricks-and-mortar showrooms and used the franchise concept in the 1890s. In 1901, Coca-Cola franchised bottling distribution (as opposed to selling its product only at soda fountains). The concept grew again with Howard Johnson hotels in the 1920s and boomed in the 1950s as consumer use of America's interstate highways expanded. In 1977 the National Alliances of Franchisees (NAF) was formed in Washington, D.C. And in 1979, FTC Rule 438 was passed requiring Uniform Franchise Offering Circular disclosures (among other things) no less than fourteen days before money changes hands in connection with a franchise purchase.

In the new economy, there is no end to the types of industries in which franchising is available, including advertising and sales, automotives, business services, child services, cleaning and maintenance services, coaching, customer service, financial and tax services, food services, home services, pet services, real estate, retail, senior care, sports and recreation, and travel and hospitality. And the best news is that the cost to open a franchise can be as little as a few thousand dollars.

Among the benefits of franchise ownership are access to proven products or services, brand name, training and support, operating and marketing methods, ongoing new products, and industry insights and other synergies—all which of result in economies of scale. This level of support can be particularly beneficial if you've never owned a business before. In theory, buying a franchise is more efficient than building your own brand and company from scratch. On the flip side are the franchise cons, including the fact that a franchise is more of a temporary business investment—you are essentially "leasing" the opportunity, not buying the business, and you are bound by a franchisor compliance agreement, often giving up certain rights.

The bottom line is that there are risks in opening any business, franchise or not. Historically, less than 5 percent of franchises close each year. That's far less than the failure rate for small businesses in general. Partially, this success relates to the level of training and support available, but also because good franchisors make sure that you're qualified before they will consider you as a franchise owner. They make more money if you succeed than if you fail. Some questions to ask if you are considering opening a franchise as a way to earn more with your fresh start strategy are included for you in the next sidebar.

Median *gross* annual income from franchise businesses in America is in the $75,000 to $124,000 range, with more than 30 percent of franchises earning over $150,000 per year. And the best part is, you are your own boss! Sure, there are plenty of things to worry about when you own your own business, but at least a pink slip isn't one of them! For more information on franchises, check out the video clip at www.askshario.com/franchising.

The Bottom Line

Americans have more "essential" expenses in the new economy than ever before, particularly as a result of technology and everybody's need to stay electronically connected in so many ways. You've learned some great ways to cut some of your "biggie" spending and strategies to ensure that tools such as loyalty and reward programs, which you think will save you money, actually do save you money. And you've learned that there are plenty of opportunities in the new economy to earn more money by pursuing second jobs or direct sales, or even by starting your own business. America was built on individualism

Fresh Start Questions:
Earning More with a Franchise

- How would owning your own business fit in with your lifestyle?

- Are you interested in a home-based or part-time business?

- Is your long-term plan to own one franchise or several?

- In what type of business interests will you feel confident, and is there a need for that type of business in your area?

- How much money do you have available to invest? Is financing available and, if so, are you comfortable with that?

- Does taking the risk make sense? Typically, there are start-up costs and ongoing fees (such as royalties for using brand names) and monthly fees that may be tied to a percentage of your gross sales.

- How does the franchisor make its money? How much will it cost you, and are the franchisor's interests aligned with yours?

- What are you getting in return for paying the franchise fee and other costs? What are you giving up? Under what circumstances can the agreement be terminated? Is there a noncompete agreement? Is your territory exclusive?

- How does the franchise compare to doing this type of business on your own?

- How much money do you believe you will potentially earn?

and hard work, and you need that exact same drive to dig deep and find ways to earn more today. This drive is what's going to take you to personal prosperity and make the country great again. Now, let's move on to some tips for getting additional help with your five-step plan, if and when you feel you need to call in professionals. And then in Chapter 8, "Paying It Forward," we'll examine how you can guarantee that your investment in education and training pays off big-time under the new economy, rules, and reforms.

PART THREE

Moving Forward

CHAPTER SEVEN

Getting the Help You Need

- **What Will You Learn from This Chapter?** You'll learn how to find a professional with the right credentials to help you navigate the new economy, rules, and reforms—someone who will work well with you at the right price. This chapter explains the wide range of different compensation packages that professionals use and teaches you how to review your bills and keep an eye out for "generous" billing. You'll learn all you need to know to maintain a beneficial experience with financial advisers.

- **How Will This Knowledge Help You?** There's no shame in needing help. In fact, it's smart business to surround yourself with sure-footed professionals who have the experience to help you make the right decisions and the empathy and dedication to fight for your cause. This chapter, together with more detailed guidance in the online Appendix, will help you find those professionals.

You will recall that in the introduction to this book we talked about the importance of the golden rules of financial fitness and responsibility. One of the rules that folks are reminded of all too often in the new economy is to be careful whom you trust. You have no doubt heard the horror stories about folks, already down on their luck, placing their trust and hard-earned money into the clutches of the wrong financial planner, stockbroker, accountant, mortgage broker, or lawyer, for example, and winding up getting royally screwed.

Adapting to the new economy, rules, and reforms often involves making seemingly monumental, and certainly difficult, decisions and changes. Admitting that you need help navigating these changes is never easy, but actually finding the right help can be even harder. On the other hand, surrounding yourself with the right advisers is one more thing that you can do to reduce the impact that the new economy's crazy variables may be having on your wallet, especially if you want to ensure a speedier, more secure fresh start path to adapting financially and prospering. You may need professional help fixing a problem, such as a modifying a home mortgage loan that you can no longer afford, or maximizing an opportunity, such as making the right business or investment decision. And timing is important. You might need proactive professional help that enables you to avoid a problem altogether, such as contemplating the tax consequences of an investment decision. Or you may need professional help dealing with a credit score dispute or debt collection issue, for example, or in defending a foreclosure lawsuit.

In any of these fresh start situations, seeking professional help at the last minute introduces the additional dynamic of imploding deadlines and time pressures that very well may make the situation even more unmanageable and stressful than it was before. That's the exact type of emotion that makes rational decision making even more difficult. Because making clear, rational choices about professional help is especially important when the stakes are high, it makes sense to avoid putting yourself in that type of worsened situation if you can. The moral of the story is, as you are reading this chapter, think about also applying the tools and tips you've learned today to help you find the right professionals that you may need *in the future.*

Keeping an Eye Out for Personal Motives

Whenever you begin a search for professional help, the one factor that should always rise to the top is "motive" and the potential for hidden conflicts between what's best for the professional you're planning to hire and what may be best for you.

When a professional represents you, it is essential to realize that his first interest and loyalty may be in representing himself, either by generating a profit or perhaps by "playing it safe," to be certain that you will have no claim of any sort against him.

Professionals who work on commission clearly have a personal incentive to get a deal done since that is how they get paid. But few people realize that even professionals who are paid a salary have a personal incentive since they are often under pressure from inside the company that they work for to generate more money. Many professionals—for example, financial planners, lawyers, bankers, and CPAs—earn salaries from their companies based on how much money they bring in from customers like you. For example, a banker may be required to meet a quota along the lines of opening at least $1 million in new deposit accounts and making at least five new loans each month. A CPA who earns $150,000 a year may be required to bring in $500,000 a year in fees. To do this, some of these professionals are sometimes required to bill for eight or ten hours of work each day! You can understand, then, how these time sheet entries may, on occasion, wind up being "estimated" by the professional.

Most professionals are wonderful folks who do care about the people they work with; however, they are in business to make money, and you represent income to them. Among other things, the fresh start tips in this chapter will help you to distinguish the professionals who do not take that personal motive to an extreme from those who do.

Decision Criteria: How to Know Which Professional Is a Good Fit for You

Your mother was right about at least one thing: You need to do your homework. Particularly when it comes to finding the right professionals to help you regain control of your financial life, a little legwork goes a long way. For starters, begin by looking for at least three potential candidates. Not only does that give you a plan B and plan C to fall back on, if your first choice does not work out, but it also allows you an important opportunity for gaining a perspective that can only come from comparing several professionals against each other. In this way, you can establish some baseline for your decision-making process. In other words, you want to get a decent idea of what the "norm" is in a given profession.

When comparing professionals, remember that you're not necessarily always looking for the smartest guy or the nicest guy or the guy with a reputation for being the top in his league. You're looking for the guy who is the best fit for you and your fresh start situation, your personality, the way you communicate, the way you like to be treated, the expectations you may have, the type and complexity of your needs, and, of course, your budget. As is often the case in life, you may not be able to find or afford everything you want in a professional, but getting clear on what it is that you're looking for is imperative—at the very least, you'll wind up with someone who possesses your essential requirements while eliminating those professionals with whom you specifically do not want to be working. In most cases it's best to begin with the ideals and then whittle down to the must-have factors.

Generally speaking, there are three basic factors that go into determining if a particular professional is the best fit for you and your fresh start plan. They are *credentials, click,* and *cost,* or the 3Cs. Let's look at each of these in more detail.

Credentials

What education, expertise, and experience does the professional need to possess?

When it comes to education, all schools and degrees are not alike. Going to a good college or other program with a solid history and reputation for providing the training relevant to a professional's area of practice is a sign that a professional is well equipped to handle your needs. Professionals who possess advanced degrees beyond the minimum requirement illustrate their personal desire to be the very best that they can be. The online Appendix has a checklist of specific questions you can take with you and ask in order to verify a professional's education.

Regarding experience, a professional's record should speak for itself. Check the results the professional has obtained for customers who needed the same kind of services that you need. Learn if he often works with a certain type or category of individual or business.

For example, if the professional you need is a trial lawyer, ask how many cases like yours he has tried, won, lost, or settled. If he's a mortgage broker and you have bad credit, ask how many customers with bad credit he's been able to help. The right professional knows what to do and acts effectively, with little wasted effort or wasted expenditure of your time and money. Questions you can bring with you and ask when you meet with a professional in order to verify his experience are also included in the online Appendix.

Click

Do you and a particular professional click or do you clash? In other words, what personality traits, communication style, method of working vs. delegating, interests, and other factors need to be present for you to work well with the professional?

Many folks overlook the importance of finding a professional they click with—someone they like, can relate to, and believe is compassionate and understanding about their situation. Remember that this person will be helping you to navigate a very important matter for you, where you are hoping to make a financial fresh start. Few things are more frustrating than paying a professional to help you and then getting the sense that he behaves as if he has more important things to do.

By hiring a professional, you are adding another person into the mix—another personality, more opinions, and a whole bundle of other human dynamics. That person shouldn't add to your problems by not caring, communicating poorly, being too aggressive or not aggressive enough, or otherwise causing a new set of challenges, including miscommunication, confusion, or delays.

In addition to personality, some of the factors that may influence how well you click with a professional adviser include the person's workload and reputation.

Workload can significantly impact a professional's ability to click with customers. Always ask how many customers or matters the professional, and each of his staff members, typically handle at any given time. Too many means that you may not get the attention you need. On the other hand, particularly if you are paying by the hour, too few may cause you to be overbilled by a professional who does not have enough work to fill up his time.

Reputation is also important. You'll want to flesh out any skeletons in the professional's closet, either by asking targeted questions of references (questions that you can ask references are covered later in this chapter) or doing some quick and simple online research. On the other hand, repeat long-term customers who return time and again over the years is a good sign.

Included in the online Appendix are specific signs and traits to look for in order to determine whether you click with a particular professional. If you can't get comfortable with someone up-front, don't expect to feel any better about him when the heat is on.

Cost

How much money will it cost to get professional help? How is the professional's compensation structured, and how are you going to pay for his services? It makes sense to do a little bit of advance legwork on the subject of cost while you are identifying the initial three candidates you will be choosing from. In this way you'll get a general idea of what you are in for and can avoid wasting time with professionals who are (to keep it simple) clearly outside of the cost range you feel is appropriate.

Start by getting a feel for the cost of the professional help you're seeking. Check websites of professionals in your area (professional service fees can vary by geographic region), or make some calls to professionals explaining that you are doing some research on cost.

Getting a rough idea about this information before you even make appointments will enable you to avoid scheduling an interview or consultation with a professional that you know for sure is outside of the norm or just plain out of your price range. Perhaps you might even decide that professional help simply isn't worth the cost. For example, if someone owes you $25,000 but the cost to sue her is $50,000 and you will not be able to recover attorney fees, a lawsuit is obviously not worthwhile pursuing. And do the math yourself. Professionals are not always going to walk away from potential fees, even if they know the results won't be worth the costs.

Now, let's plunge into more detail into exactly how professionals are paid, and how you can keep those payments reasonable.

How Professionals Are Paid

How do most professionals charge for their services? Professionals such as Realtors, mortgage brokers, and some financial planners are typically paid a portion of what you pay for real estate, a mortgage, or investments. Lawyers, CPAs, and other professionals may be paid hourly fees or have some other arrangement. But in all cases the money is coming out of your pocket. Here's a simple explanation of the more common professional compensation arrangements.

Retainers

In the context of professional compensation, the word *retainer* can mean one of two things. The first definition for retainer is a regular ongoing sum of money sometimes paid to keep a professional available to provide you with his services. For example, a bank might keep a construction consultant on retainer to oversee development projects the bank is financing by paying him $1,000 per month. The second meaning can be a deposit or down payment paid to a professional and typically held in an escrow or trust account, to be applied against the professional's fees, which are earned later. This second meaning is more common and is more likely to be what a professional will be referring to if he asks you to pay him a retainer. The retainer is simply a professional's safety net or buffer to make sure that you pay his fees.

If you are asked to pay a retainer that you cannot afford or feel is excessive, do not hesitate to negotiate. You may be able to pay the retainer over time, or ask to be billed more frequently (for example, twice a month instead of once a month) so that the professional doesn't have to be quite as concerned that you might not pay his bill. Retainers are most common with lawyers, CPAs, financial planners, and in cases where the professional will have to pay some out-of-pocket expenses for services to third parties up-front, for your benefit.

Hourly Fees

There will be times when you need fresh start help, but the professional will not be able to predict exactly the amount of time that he will need to dedicate to helping you. In such cases, the professional may want to charge you by the hour. This is the most common type of fee structure for CPAs, lawyers, and some financial planners. Since not every professional charges the same amount per hour, it is critical that you ask for the professional's hourly rate. The answer should include the hourly rate for the professional, as well as the hourly rates charged for the professional's support staff—associates, secretaries, and on-staff experts, consultants, or other service providers. Hourly rates vary widely depending on the type of work, the professional's level of experience and training, and even the professional's geographic location (since office rental and other costs vary by geography and, at the end of the day, these overhead costs get passed through to you in the professional's hourly rate).

The dollar amount of a professional's hourly rate doesn't mean everything. Some professionals may charge more per hour but are able to get your job done quicker or more efficiently. In other words, you may pay a higher hourly rate but end up spending less overall in the long run. So, in addition to the rate, you will also want to know approximately how many hours the professional estimates will be involved in completing your matter. Most professionals will be hesitant to commit to a definite number but should be able to give you a range or at least a "best-case" and "worst-case" scenario. Also, be sure to ask if you will be charged for *all* of the professional's time *all* of the time. For example, some professionals charge for every single e-mail and telephone call, no matter how brief, while others do not. And, if the matter at hand is some sort of transaction—for example, maybe you are buying or selling real estate or a business— remember that the professional's fees may still be due even if your deal falls through and is not consummated; however, you may be able to negotiate up-front to pay a reduced amount should that happen.

If you hire a professional based on an hourly fee arrangement, you are probably going to want to do what you can to keep the professional's billable hours, and therefore your costs, down without compromising the expertise and service you get. The quick tips in the sidebar will help you to do just that.

One-Minute Mentor:
Quick Tips for Keeping Fees Down When You Are Paying a Professional by the Hour

BE UP-FRONT

Always be candid, up-front, and honest about all of the facts when you communicate with the professional. At the end of the day the full story will come out. The longer it takes to get there, the more it will cost you. And if your professional unwittingly acts on false or incomplete information, it could lead to even bigger problems you need to fresh start.

BE PREPARED

Always take a few moments to prepare in advance for telephone calls and in-person meetings with the professional. Ask in advance if there's anything new that you should bring, and take the initiative yourself to bring photocopies of all relevant documents to the meetings with your professional. Also, write the questions you want to ask the professional down in advance of every telephone call or meeting, and keep them brief.

BE SUCCINCT

Be straightforward and to the point in all of your communication with the professional. Don't get emotional or ramble. Ask up-front which details and information matter and which don't so that you will know what to filter. What are the elements that you will need to provide? Then focus on those elements.

SAVE IT UP

Don't call or e-mail every time you think of something you want to ask or tell the professional. Instead, keep a notepad handy and save up your thoughts so that you can deliver them in one telephone call or e-mail. This will enable the professional to handle your thoughts, questions, and concerns as efficiently (and inexpensively) as possible.

Flat Fees

Sometimes a professional may be willing to work for a "fixed" or "flat" fee. Matters that lend themselves to fixed or flat-fee structures tend to be less complicated. In those matters, professionals hope to make money from a large volume of similar cases and, perhaps, lower overhead. Examples may include negotiating a mortgage loan modification, preparing a simple tax return, or negotiating a payment plan for your credit card. You should realize that while the potentially lower cost of a flat-fee professional service might seem appealing, it may not provide you with the most customized, responsive type of service. If you need a lot of hand-holding, a flat-fee structure is not for you. One other caveat: Beware of "add-ons" with fixed or flat-fee service providers. Extra fees for things like photocopies, use of a conference room, or long-distance telephone calls are sometimes a backhanded way to recover professional time incurred above and beyond what might initially be expected.

If a professional won't work for a fixed or flat fee, ask if he will consider capping his fee so that you can at least budget for the worst-case scenario. Sometimes, even this option is not possible, because while you and the professional may have some control over how much time your fresh start matter will require, there may still be variables beyond the control of either of you. If the answer is "no" to a fee cap, you can ask to be notified if and when the cost begins to exceed a specific threshold so that you can consider a strategy change or at least not be surprised when a bill much bigger than what you're expecting arrives in the mail.

Contingency Fees

Contingency fee structures, in which the professional will not receive payment unless you prevail in the matter you hire him to handle, are most commonly seen in certain types of lawsuits, debt collections, or sometimes in tax refund disputes, particularly if you present a very strong case and the other side clearly has the money to pay you (or, as professionals say, it's "collectable"). But you can also creatively utilize the contingency fee structure in less traditional contexts.

In a nutshell, the contingency fee will be a percentage of the money that you collect. Professionals with midsize companies tend to be more open to contingency fee arrangements, for several reasons. First, bigger companies tend to have higher overhead and are less willing to take the risk of a contingency fee. At smaller companies, on the other hand, contingency fee matters can likewise be tough, because it's expensive for smaller companies to pay professionals while they work on a contingency fee matter without generating any income for the company. Where contingency fees are concerned, a company is essentially "financing" the matter until it's resolved. Tips for negotiating contingency fees and important laws concerning contingency fees can be found in the online Appendix.

Remember, if you can't find anyone to take your matter on a contingency basis, it may be because you don't have a matter worthwhile pursuing, either because the other side is not "collectable" or the costs that the matter will involve just don't make business sense because the potential win (or "upside") is simply too small. All are good reasons for you to consider not proceeding with the matter in the first place.

Commission

Again, some professionals, including some financial planners, stockbrokers and insurance brokers, Realtors, and mortgage brokers, are most often paid by commission. A commission is typically a percentage of the price of whatever it is that is being purchased, sold, or managed. For example, a Realtor may be paid 6 percent of the price she sells your home for. A stockbroker may be paid one percent of the price of the stock she buys on your behalf. A financial planner may be paid 2 percent of the value of the investment portfolio she manages for you. Others may be paid based on a combination of hourly rates, fixed or flat fees, and commission. Paying a professional based on commission presents some unique potential for conflicts, which is discussed further in the online Appendix.

Free, Discount, and Subsidized Professional Help

When it comes to professionals, hiring the best of the best can be expensive. But, as you know, you won't always need the best of the best. Sometimes you will merely need to get the job done. Under those circumstances, you may sometimes be able to find a professional who can meet your needs just as well through a free, discount fee, or subsidized service. HUD-certified counselors and Legal Aid lawyers are two examples of free or discounted professional services. In fact, the Department of Housing and Urban Development provides free and discounted counseling and training in a multitude of areas relevant to your five fresh start steps, including debt management budgeting; rental housing; homebuying, homeownership, and home improvement; predatory lending; and reverse mortgages (see the online video at www.askshario.com/counseling). Don't expect cutting-edge turnaround time or concierge-style service from free, discounted, or subsidized professionals. They typically have their hands full, and they don't take on all cases, but you can still qualify them by following the 3Cs.

If your situation is particularly unfortunate, or your particular matter is newsworthy, or if you're lucky enough to otherwise convince someone to help you, you may find yourself working with a professional who volunteers to help folks who can't afford to pay full price for her services—for example, a "pro bono" lawyer. However, remember that a pro bono professional also has paying clients who must be taken care of, and who will sometimes take priority over you, so that her own bills can get paid.

Getting Comfortable with Professional Fee and Service Agreements

A written agreement is imperative anytime you hire or engage a professional. This can be a document you actually sign or simply a letter from the professional that sets forth the specific services he will provide for you, the compensation he will receive in return, when, and from whom. In fact, under many circumstances, professionals are actually required by law to provide you with a written agreement. It goes without saying, and you will recall it's one of the golden rules, that you need to be sure you understand any legal agreement completely before you sign it. Don't be afraid to ask the professional to explain it, or to even make changes. It is critical that you get off on the right foot with this important relationship. If you are not comfortable asking basic questions from the beginning, don't walk, run away and find someone you are more comfortable communicating with.

Strategies for Finding the Right Professional

Now that you know what it is that you are looking for in a professional, what is the smartest way to actually go about finding the right guy or gal for your needs? This section covers the five most common strategies for discovering the best service professional for you.

Personal Referrals

As with hiring any other important service provider, one of the best ways to locate a professional to help you with your fresh start plan, if it is possible, is by asking folks you know and trust for a referral. Remember, however, that many referral sources have their own personal motives that may not be completely aligned with what's in your best interest. A friend may recommend "the best banker in the galaxy," which turns out to be that friend's brother-in-law (and, as it turns out, your friend actually never banked with him). Sometimes, the folks you may ask for referrals are not even completely conscious of their own personal motives. To clarify the motives of your referral sources, ask some questions.

Four Simple Questions for Uncovering Hidden Motives

1. How did you come to know this professional?

2. What is the relationship between you and this professional?

3. Exactly what professional experience have you had with this professional?

4. Specifically, why are you endorsing this particular professional?

Professional Referrals

One of the best ways to find professionals with a top-notch reputation for a particular type of work is to ask other professionals in the same community. After all, the best professionals typically know the people they would hire for themselves. Often, that's the guy *you* want to hire, too. So if you're looking for a bankruptcy lawyer, ask the divorce lawyer you know (or that your best friend knows) for a referral. Of course, don't forget the four simple questions for uncovering hidden motives. Remember, some professionals are financially compensated, directly or indirectly, for making referrals and, as you know, they're only human.

Professional Rating and Referral Services

Many professions have their own systems for evaluating and rating members of their own profession, but use these sources with care. Many professional rating and referral sources do not provide some of the more candid insights in terms of credentials, click, and cost. And many of these services have their own motives, such as charging a fee for professionals to be listed or sometimes even earning a fee for referrals. Nevertheless, professional rating services can help you compare several professionals against each other.

If you do plan to use a rating or referral service, always find out how the ratings are determined, how they decide which professionals to recommend, and exactly how the service works.

Professional Associations

Most professionals have associations that guide and govern them. For example, lawyers have the American Bar Association, as well as state and local bar associations. Mortgage brokers and bankers likewise have national, state, and local associations, as do CPAs, financial planners, and others. These organizations typically have websites and even member directories containing the names of current members, as well as the organization's officers, committee members, and heads. State bar associations and other professional associations also may have specialty "certifications" that members of that profession can earn. A certification usually requires a professional to have practiced in that area of expertise for a certain number of years, to have studied for and passed an exam, and to participate in continuing education every few years designed to keep certified professionals up to speed on all the newest developments and information in their field—to essentially keep them at the "top of their game."

Professional associations and their websites are great resources for finding great professionals, as well as for verifying credentials and eliminating the bad guys. If you can't find exactly what you're looking for, don't hesitate to call the association itself or even the committee members or officers. These folks are often the professionals who organize or speak at educational programs in their field and are in an excellent position to suggest the names of professional candidates they know who may fit your needs. Again, don't forget to ask the four simple questions about motivation to qualify any referral that they may make.

Online Research

Prominent professionals who have taken on challenging and difficult cases in their fields of expertise are often regularly mentioned in general circulation newspapers as well as professional publications. If you have access to a computer and your local newspaper is online, you may want to run a newspaper search for the type of professional that you are looking for. Obviously, you can also look for a professional's own website, but these sources are essentially high-tech advertisements.

If you can't find a professional any other way, advertisements—whether online or more traditional print advertisements—are last resorts. Just remember that you will need to interview professionals found in this manner even more judiciously. In those situations where you do find yourself placing heavy reliance on an advertisement, remember to ask how much of the professional's business is generated by his advertising and how much comes from referrals, then decide for yourself if his answer may be a red flag.

Vetting the Three Professional Candidates You Identify

When it comes to vetting professionals, there is no substitute for a face-to-face meeting, and it's important that this meeting take place at the professional's place of business. You will not only find it easier to confirm whether a professional has the necessary credentials, but also it will be easier to know whether you click with a professional and could form a comfortable working relationship with him. Meeting at the professional's office will provide you with important insights, not the least of which is a behind-the-scenes glance at how well his office and staff seem to function. It is not uncommon for folks to sometimes feel a bit awkward or even intimidated about asking for a preliminary interview or initial consultation with a professional. Most often, this is simply a matter of the fear of the unknown, but sometimes it also has to do with the feeling that you may be imposing, or you may have difficulty asking for help because you feel embarrassed about having gotten yourself into an undesirable situation in the first place where you now need a fresh start.

Obviously, you can't just show up at a professional's office and expect this person to see you. Instead, the first step is to call each of the three candidates on your short list and ask if they would be available to be interviewed about handling your matter and whether they would charge you for this initial consultation time.

Calling for an Appointment

When you call a professional's office for an appointment, be prepared to describe your situation in twenty words or less. Remember that in that first phone call you will be talking to a receptionist or other administrative person who is not the expert; thus any details or facts, other than the basics, are irrelevant and may easily be misunderstood or miscommunicated. Also, just as you will be vetting the professional, so will the professional be vetting you as a potential customer. The purpose of this telephone call is merely to establish a date and time to meet and give the professional a general idea of what the meeting will be about. Now is not the time to drop a boatload of information or to try to get information, answers, or solutions to your problem. Folks who try those tactics risk coming across as flaky, emotional, and potentially high maintenance. A third reason for avoiding details is confidentiality. Considering that you may not end up working with this firm, now is not the time to share with administrative and other staff the confidential details of your situation.

Preparing to Meet the Professional

Just as you prepared yourself prior to making the initial telephone call to schedule your appointment with the professional, you must also do preparation before attending your initial consultation. Specifically, prepare a one-page summary of your fresh start facts, your needs, and the outcome that you desire, including any dates, dollar amounts, times, and names/addresses relevant to your situation. Provide the basic who, what, where, when, why, and how information. Make photocopies of all relevant documents that help to tell, support, or prove your story. If your situation is one that makes you feel particularly angry, sad, or frustrated, for example, be sure to carefully review a draft of your one-page summary, highlighting any of the information you've included that may be perceived as being more emotional than factual, then consider removing it from your summary. Professionals meet with dozens of people, each with his own fresh start "story," and many of these people feel they have been "wronged." Judges, creditors, banks, the IRS, and others with whom the professional may eventually be dealing on your behalf will not care about anything other than the numbers, the law, or the facts. Accordingly, at least during the initial consultation, it is best to first share only the facts with a professional. A handy checklist to help prepare for initial consultations with specific types of professionals, including what to take with you to that appointment, is included in the online Appendix.

Arriving at the Initial Professional Consultation

It's advisable to arrive at an initial consultation appointment with a professional approximately fifteen minutes early. If there are other folks in the reception room, don't be shy. Ask if they've been happy with the professional's work. Take along the checklist of "Questions to Ask a Reference" (provided in the online Appendix) and ask everyone the same questions. (If you feel the need, practice these questions in advance so that you're more comfortable asking them.) Understandably, some folks you meet may not want to discuss specific details about their own situations; after all, that information may be personal. But as long as you stick to a general discussion about the professional's 3Cs, you'll find that most people will not consider the conversation to be prying and are happy to help and share their opinions while they wait with you for their own appointments.

While you're waiting, also observe how the professional's office staff seems to be functioning. Are they happy? Do they work well together? When the telephone rings, do they seem eager to answer it or are they behaving as if those telephone calls from other customers are nothing more than an annoying interruption? Do they seem to be working hard, focused, organized? Are they polite to the other customers and to each other? Are they being properly supervised? How does the office itself appear? Fancy? Messy? Neat and clean? Modern or dated? A checklist to take along for an initial consultation appointment with a professional, designed to help you remember what to look for while you are waiting, is included for you in the online Appendix.

When your appointment time arrives, does the professional greet you for your appointment on time? Does she take the time that you feel is appropriate to get to know you and your needs, or does she make you feel rushed? Do you have her undivided attention, or is she looking at e-mails and taking telephone calls while you're meeting with her? Is the professional someone you can relate to? Are there perhaps awards or plaques from groups that you also support or belong to, or are there indications that you have other things in common with this person? Check out diplomas on the walls to help vet credentials. All of these cues can give you insight into what a professional and her staff would be like for you to work with should you choose to become a customer. The online Appendix includes a checklist of nonverbal cues you can observe about the professional, so you'll be more informed before you make your decision.

The Initial Professional Interview or Consultation

The general questions you will want to ask at an initial consultation that apply to virtually all types of professionals and situations are included for you here. You will find that they all relate to the 3Cs: credentials, "click" factor, and costs.

Taking Advantage of a Second Set of Eyes and Ears

Sometimes it feels as if there's a lot to take in all at once at an initial consultation with a professional. If you are already feeling anxious or don't trust your own instincts completely, you may want to consider bringing a close friend or family member along with you to the initial consultation with a professional. After all, two sets of eyes and ears, observations, and opinions are always better than one. Sometimes when you're nervous or focusing on the questions that you need to ask a professional, the person you bring along may be better able to pick up on cues that you might otherwise miss.

Staff

Many professionals work with others (partners, employees, and associates), so it is important to know what the qualifications of these other people are, too. Ask about their level of involvement in handling your business. Ask to meet the staff who will assist with your matter during your initial consultation. Remember that when you are in a hospital, you may see the doctor once a day, but the nurses provide the hourly care. The same is often true in the professional office environment. Professionals perform direct services, but they also give instructions and orders to others. Their qualifications and your "click" factor with these other folks may be just as important as your assessment of the professional herself.

Strategy

What will be the professional's process or approach to your situation? Be wary of professionals who are long on assurances but short on concrete steps or timelines. And steer clear of professionals who "guarantee" certain results. After the real estate bubble burst, millions of folks learned the hard way that when something sounds too good to be true, it probably is.

Decision Making

Determine how and at what point(s) you and the professional will agree to proceed. Does the professional tend to make these decisions, or will he be sharing decision making with you? If it's a lawyer or CPA you're working with, for example, does she have settlement authority? If it's a mortgage banker, can he lock in an interest rate for you? Will you be able to approve all e-mails and letters before they are sent? Remember, if you're working with the type of professional who may agree to provide services for a contingency fee, flat fee, or a fee cap, she may have a personal incentive to spend as little time as possible on the assignment and wrap up your business quickly and make decisions accordingly, which may conflict with what's best for you.

Professional Liability

Does the professional (or the company she works for) carry adequate professional liability insurance? Has she ever been sued, lost clients, or had a professional complaint filed against her? If so, how many times, and what were the reasons and the outcomes? No professional should be offended by questions of this nature if you explain that you are bringing up these unlikely possibilities so that you can gain some assurance that you can trust her completely.

References

Toward the end of the initial consultation is when you will generally ask a professional to provide the names and telephone numbers or e-mail addresses for at least three references you can contact in order to get a better feel for how well suited the professional is for you and your need. Of course, the unspoken word, if you read between the lines, is that you will also be verifying with these references the accuracy and completeness of everything that the professional has told you. Because current customers have not yet completed the full experience of working with a professional and do not yet know how their matters will conclude, and because they have a motive to "not make waves" with the professional that might impact their own matters, it's prudent to ask for at least one reference who is a former customer. As is the case with referral sources, don't forget to flesh out whatever personal motives or conflicts a reference may have (see again the "Four Simple Questions for Uncovering Hidden Motives" behind referrals, in the previous section on Strategies for Finding the Right Professional).

It's also advisable to ensure that the professional has permission from each reference to give you his name, so ask the professional to call or send an e-mail to each reference, copying you, so that each reference knows that you will be contacting him.

When you do contact these references, ask targeted questions designed to verify the professional's 3Cs: Revisit the sections on credentials, click, and cost for examples of the issues you want to ask about when you contact references. Always thank the reference and ask if it would be okay for you to contact him again should any further questions arise.

Money

Finally, if you are satisfied with the professional's credentials and click, it's time to address cost. The online Appendix has a checklist of questions to ask about fees that you can take along with you on an initial consultation with a professional.

Let's face it, talking about money with anyone can be uncomfortable. With a professional service provider in particular, you may worry about offending him by inadvertently implying that you don't think he's worth the money. Or you may end up embarrassing yourself by seeming naïve or perhaps appearing as if you can't afford to pay for his services. The relationships folks have with money in general can be complicated. Getting comfortable talking about money is an important step in unraveling those emotions and taking control of your financial life. Putting this anxiety to rest in the context of your conversations with a professional you are considering hiring is easy.

Evaluating the Three Professional Candidates You Interview

After each consultation with a candidate professional, take a moment to reflect on the 3Cs. How do this professional's *credentials* compare to what you think you need and with those of the other professionals you've met with? Did you *click*? What was your overall comfort level with this person? Did the professional give you clear and direct information? Did he answer your questions? Does his preferred method for communicating match your own preferences? Are you comfortable with how often you can expect to hear from him? Did he speak knowledgeably and steer clear of overly technical terms? Do you believe that he will be available in an emergency? And last but not least, does the *cost* of his service fit in with what you had budgeted and what you have learned is normal? If you are paying by the hour, someone who likes to hear himself talk can translate into bigger costs. Also, sometimes professionals use technical talk to conceal the fact that they don't really know an answer. For a true professional, ensuring that you understand what he is saying, not impressing you with big words, is the top priority.

Keeping Informed: The Importance of Good Communication and Follow-Up

In addition to keeping costs down, good communication will help ensure that your expectations are met and that you get what you want and need from a professional. As is the case with any other interpersonal relationship, good communication works both ways. Be equally clear about what your own responsibilities are and be sure to live up to them. At the end of the day, whatever your fresh-start challenge is that a professional may be working on for you, it is still *your* responsibility or *your* opportunity. The professional is only helping you with it. You are the CEO of your own destiny. The professionals you hire merely work for you. As such, ultimately, it is up to you to stay on top of things and follow up.

Some folks hire a professional and then "check out" for a variety of reasons. Sometimes they think they no longer have to be involved. Other times, they just don't want to deal with it. While you don't want to irritate a professional and risk driving up his time and your cost with frequent telephone calls and e-mails, you also don't want to disappear off the face of the earth. A telephone call or e-mail every now and then can be a useful way of letting the professional know that you are keeping an eye on the matter; in this way, too, you may perhaps jog his memory about something he's been meaning to tell or ask you. Certainly, communication can only help keep you aware of what is going on and help you know if an obstacle emerges, enabling you to take corrective steps before it gets out of control. Even if a professional came highly recommended or you've worked well with him before, don't take it for granted that he will always be on top of your situation the way you would like him to be. Things change. You never know when a professional may be going through his own personal hardships, staff shortages, or simple burnout. Any of these variables could easily impact how well your problem is handled.

Do not expect to always be able to accomplish immediate communication with a professional by telephone. Professionals are frequently tied up or out of the office. They have meetings with other customers and professionals, even appearances in court or other places. They may not be available to accept your telephone call right away for a variety of reasons. Depending on the frequency of communication that your issue calls for, regularly scheduled face-to-face meetings or telephone conferences are one alternative that may meet both the professional's and your needs. Scheduled appointments will help you avoid telephone tag and increase the probability of a successful exchange of information on a regular, periodic basis. Ask to be copied on correspondence and documents that the professional sends and receives on your behalf. If you do not understand what they mean, save those questions for your next scheduled meeting or telephone call.

Again, it's helpful to think of your professional as you would think of your doctor. After you see a physician, he might order tests or take some other action and ask you to come back at some future time. It's up to you to follow through and schedule the next appointment. Follow the same practice with your financial professional and always end each communication by clarifying the next time that you should expect to touch base for follow-up.

Communicating any questions or concerns about a professional's bills in a timely manner will also make life easier for both of you.

Fresh Start Tips for Reviewing Your Bills

If you are going to be paying a professional by the hour, or even based on a fixed, flat, or capped fee, you will want to carefully review the professional's bills as soon as you can after they arrive in the mail.

In the big picture, the primary reason for carefully reviewing a professional's bill is to make sure that your matter is being properly staffed with the right number and the right type of people. Particularly if you're paying a professional by the hour, too many people with their hands in the mix can quickly translate to an excessive bill. Underqualified staffing means you may wind up paying for folks to learn on the job. You'll want to be sure to review all of your professional bills as soon as you get them, while things are still fresh in your mind. For example, are you being billed for multiple internal meetings involving multiple staff? You have the right to question these charges. Be aware of the potential to overuse fluff-sounding descriptions like "analyze," "review," and "strategize." A professional's bills should be specific and detailed in time entries. Junior professionals, in particular, should not be doing "big-picture" work. Is unnecessary staff being paid (by you!) to read e-mails or documents on which they did not need to be cc'd? It's always a good idea to insist on meeting everybody who will be billing you for their time so that you can answer these questions. For these and other items to watch out for in your professional's bill, see the online Appendix.

One final word on professional service bills: Always pay your bill on time, especially if you are satisfied with the work being done for you. If you have questions, address them right away. Professionals resent having to hound clients for money. It is time-consuming and uncomfortable. On top of that, if you are working with a company, the amount of time that it takes for a customer to pay a professional's bill may be factored into a professional's annual review and compensation. If someone is doing a good job for you, it's only right that you do good by him, too.

Spotting the Scammers

Scam artists have been around since the beginning of time. No one, no matter how rich or poor, is immune. Think Bernie Madoff, Allen Stanford, Marc Dreier, Scott Rothstein, and the host of others in the past few years. (In fact, the phrase *Ponzi scheme* is named after an actual Italian scam artist named Carlo Ponzi, going back to the early twentieth century.) Back during the more recent bubble when money was flowing like water, scammers focused on folks' lack of attention to detail and their tendency to "look the other way" or believe the seemingly unbelievable—tendencies that irrational exuberance and greed seem to breed. Most of the folks who entrusted Bernard Madoff, for example, never even asked specifically how he was making unbelievable amounts of money for them.

Conversely, common scams in the new economy, including credit repair scams, foreclosure rescue, and mortgage- or real estate–related frauds, tend to take advantage of desperation and the problems folks are now facing. Downward trends in the economy, employment, and real estate, taken together, provide an ideal climate for fraudsters to prey on folks when they are most vulnerable. In either case, learning to spot the scam artists—particularly when they are disguised as professionals like Realtors, mortgage brokers, bankers, CPAs, financial planners, stockbrokers, credit counselors, modification consultants, and appraisers, for example—is a critical component of knowing how to get financial help without getting taken. Some of the more common scams proliferating in specific professions today, along with tips for spotting them, are included in the online Appendix. For more information, see the video clip at www.askshario.com/spottingscammers.

Want to Know More?

If you want to know more about finding the right professional help for you, the following tips (and corresponding videos) are provided for you in the online Appendix:

Insiders Secrets for Finding the Best Financial Planner— www.askshario.com/bestplanner

Insider Secrets for Finding the Best Stockbroker

Insider Secrets for Finding the Best Accountant

Insider Secrets for Finding the Best Bookkeeper

Insider Secrets for Finding the Best Banker— www.askshario.com/bestbanker

Insider Secrets for Finding the Best Mortgage Broker— www.askshario.com/bestbroker

Insider Secrets for Finding the Best Mortgage Modification Consultant

Insider Secrets for Finding the Best Realtor— www.askshario.com/realtor

Insider Secrets for Finding the Best Lawyer— www.askshario.com/bestattorney

Insider Secrets for Finding the Best Insurance Agent

Insider Secrets for Finding the Best Mental Health Professional

Insider Secrets for Finding the Best Housing Counselor and Credit Repair and Debt Manager

Now that we know you can get the best help should you need without getting taken, there is no stopping you.

CHAPTER EIGHT

Paying It Forward: Education, Training, and Your Future Prosperity

- **What Will You Learn from This Chapter?** This chapter clearly connects the dots between your investment in education and training and the return on that investment, in terms of your employment, wages, and upward mobility, which is, after all, what your financial fresh start is all about.

- **How Will This Know-How Help You?** If you're struggling to make ends meet or to achieve upward mobility, this knowledge will help you identify concrete education and training strategies for making a fresh start that will lead to a sustainable career in any economy.

Then and Now:
Education and Employment Under the New Economy, Rules, and Reforms

Up until a few decades ago, average job duration for many Americans was almost twenty years. Usually, folks got a job right out of whatever level of school or training they'd completed and pretty much kept that job, or at least jobs very much like it, until they retired. Technology played a smaller role and relationships and personal service a larger one. In fact, many companies used to reflect a model of "labor hoarding" where, even when demand was down, employers held on to employees, at least in part out of loyalty or simply to be certain that they would have enough help when things picked up again. At the end of the day, long-term employer–employee relationships could be called a "given" that worked both ways.

If you fast-forward to the new economy, you'll see an entirely different norm. Over two-thirds of baby boomers work less than five years at a given job and, even before the Great Recession, for Gen Xers, job duration was only about half of that. If you play by the old "rules," today you'll likely be left in the dust because the rules of the employment game in the new economy have dramatically changed. If, on the other hand, you want to prosper when others do not, here's one thing about jobs that you need to know: In the new economy, employers have adapted a model best described as a far more cost-conscious, "in the nick of time" approach to hiring, essentially hiring as and when their customers' needs go up and then immediately laying off when demand goes down again. The goal for most employers in the new economy is to squeeze more productivity out of the employees that they do keep and avoid committing to permanent hires for as long as they possibly can. For employers, this arrangement translates to less risk and more profit. For unprepared employees, it translates to a higher likelihood of unemployment, less earnings, skepticism, and distrust.

Even if you are fortunate enough *not* to be one of the millions of discouraged, unemployed, or underemployed Americans competing for as few as one new job opening for every seven job seekers, the new economy reality you must contemplate is that over a forty- or fifty-year career, for example, you may wind up changing jobs more than a dozen times. On top of that, you learned in Chapter 1 that American workers' wages have not kept pace with other economic indicators. Even when times have not been tough, prosperity for folks with a high school diploma or less has grown increasingly more difficult. In 1970, 95 percent of jobs were held by men who did not have more than a high school diploma. Their medium earnings were approximately $50,000. By 2010, high school graduates accounted for 70 percent of working men, and the median salary had plunged to $25,000! It used to be that honest, hard work was rewarded with financial success. But in the new economy, getting a fresh start in education, training, and employment is no longer just an "academic" discussion; in the new economy, it's a matter of survival.

The Number-One Obstacle: Considering Costs

Of course, as much as we want to improve our potential for employment reliability, earnings, and upward mobility, the other side of the training and education investment equation is the cost, including both the cost of tuition and the opportunity cost (in other words, the income that you cannot be out earning while you are being trained or educated and not working full-time). Cost is, hands down, the number-one obstacle for most folks when it comes to being able to (or not being able to) access education or training. In the new economy, 94 percent of people pursuing a bachelor's degree borrow money from the federal government, private lenders, or relatives to do so, almost double the number of students that borrowed money only fifteen years ago. This is not surprising given the steadily increasing price of a university education—between 1981 and today, the average cost of tuition at a four-year public university rose eightfold.

"Investing" in Your Education and Training Fresh Start: Balancing Costs, Risks, and Return on Investment

Because cost is a fundamental factor in education and training, it may be helpful if you view whatever money you are contemplating spending or borrowing for education or training the same way that you would view money that you spend or borrow for an investment in general. For reasons that will be explained shortly, it is no longer prudent for you to assume that any education is worth the money, or to simply choose an educational institution because it's convenient, or a field of study merely because it sounds interesting. Instead, as is the case with the investments covered in Chapter 4, all investments in education or training are not equal. They vary by cost, risk, and potential return on investment. As you will see in the next section, some levels, fields, and types of schools or programs actually provide you with a higher likelihood of quicker or more consistent employment, higher demand, better wages, and an increased likelihood for promotion. Voilà, upward mobility!

Simply put, your education and training fresh start goal is to match the lowest investment risk and cost with the highest return on that investment, hopefully in a career that you will enjoy. Be forewarned, some of the institutions whose job it is to sell you education and training may encourage you to ignore these essential business factors. But not to worry, this chapter provides you with the basic tools that you will need to protect yourself and your future prosperity as your education, training, and employment fresh start plan unfolds.

Let's begin by looking at the cost side of the education equation: the *investment* required to pay for the education and training necessary for success in today's economy. As costs go up and jobs are more scarce, the benefit side of the equation—the return on that investment in terms of better employment opportunities and higher salaries—decreases. Then we'll take a look at some of the ways you can increase the benefit resulting from an investment in education by carefully choosing the right education *levels* and *fields* of study and training.

New Economy Challenges: The Cost Side of Your Education Equation

Even as the cost of education and training soars, education and training remains a good lifetime investment—only nowadays it comes with an unprecedented financial burden and at a time when employment and wages to repay a student loan are harder to come by. In fact, the average student loan debt amounts to just under $25,000, and the current balance of federal student loans nationwide adds up to almost $1 trillion, with almost another $150 billion in private student loans. This represents an increase that far exceeds other types of debt.

Four notable dynamics impact the cost of education and training in the new economy: (1) the increasing cost of tuition, (2) the deceasing ability to pay for an education, (3) decreasing help available from government, and (4) the growth of "for-profit" education.

Increasing Cost of Education

First, as growth in American worker wages began to slow decades ago, the cost of education began rising, in many cases faster than family incomes. And even since, the cost of tuition and fees has continued to increase faster than the rate of inflation. Some of this increase is the result of additional services and enhanced facilities, but a large part is due to federal and state budget cuts, discussed further shortly.

Decreasing Ability to Pay for the Cost of Education

Second, home equity has historically served as an important resource Americans relied on to help fund the cost of education and training. However, during this same period, Americans have increasingly relied on the equity in their homes to cover other financial shortfalls, reducing the equity available to help pay for education and training. And of course, in the new economy, many folks are without home equity altogether and even underwater. Figure 8-1 illustrates how the cost of tuition has grown at more than twice the rate of home values and earnings in general.

Decreasing Help from The America Company

Third, more than 70 percent of students attend public educational institutions. You'll recall, Chapter 1 explained how big government spending, debt, and deficits eventually come out of your pocket one way or another. Well, this is an example of one of those ways. When tough choices have to be made, education, which falls under "discretionary spending," is often on the chopping block as political leaders know that other funding sources will be found—namely, taxpayers like you! Over the past decade, as enrollment at state colleges and universities has grown, states are somewhat counterintuitively

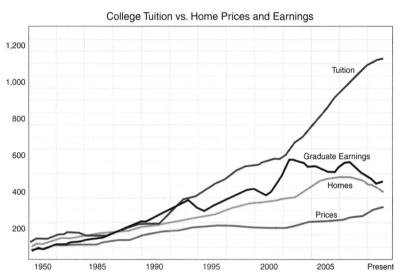

Figure 8-1. The cost of education has increased faster than the average American's ability to pay for it

cutting, rather than increasing, their spending for education. As other costs (like pensions covered in Chapter 4) grow out of control, many states have simply not budgeted enough money to keep up with this growing number of students. That trend is further accelerated by shrinking state budgets thanks to the Great Recession. In fact, spending per student has reached a twenty-five-year low. Over the past decade, state and local financing per student has declined by almost 25 percent, as Washington has increasingly pulled back on funding in order to meet other growing budget needs of The America Company. The historically held belief that state-subsidized education is an affordable stepping-stone for America's lower and middle classes is now officially at risk.

Together, these trends translate to increases in tuition and the need for students to borrow more money.

Growth of For-Profit Education

Fourth, aggressive marketing and recruiting by for-profit educators and trainers has doubled enrollment in that type of institution (also enhancing the attention that Wall Street pays to these organizations). More recently, for-profit educational lenders have been compared to pre-bubble subprime mortgage brokers. Students complain that they were encouraged to borrow more money and were misled about costs, and that their potential job prospects (the returns that they would be able to get on their investment) were exaggerated. In fact, government reports and lawsuits have accused some for-profit colleges of outright fraud. In the new economy, more than 10 percent of students attend for-profit educational and training institutions and receive a remarkable 25 percent of federal student loans and grants. At the same time, these institutions serve a valuable need

The cost-benefit analysis when it comes to education and training has been further complicated by seemingly continual tuition increases, a vast array of grants and loans, and a financial aid system that discounts tuition for most students based on opaque formulas, further obscuring the costs.

As a result, the new rules and reforms now require that educational institutions disclose certain information clearly on their websites including price of attendance, retention rate, graduate rate (for example, fewer than one in three students who go to a community college have completed a program three years later, exponentially increasing cost and decreasing benefit), job placement for graduates, and a net cost calculator.

Words from the Wise: Fresh Start Tips for Borrowing to Cover Education and Training Costs

Jennifer Anglin, president of Allied Health Institute, a for-profit institution educating and training students in the healthcare industries, offers this advice:

"Students should visit the Integrated Postsecondary Education Data System (IPEDS) website [http://nces.ed.gov/ipeds/ and select College Navigator]. IPEDS provides basic information on postsecondary institutions. Students will be able to find institutions and compare them side by side. They will be able to review student enrollments, tuition, student expenses, graduation rates, tuition, financial aid, default rate, average loan amount, and average grant amount. Students who have loan repayments and cannot find employment should request forbearance on their school loan. Student should never default on their student loan for nonpayment. Students should contact lenders for assistance in reducing payment or placing the loan in forbearance status. Students should be aware of the statutory and regulatory requirements of gainful employment. When a student graduates with student loans, if the student has to spend most of his or her income paying back the loan, is the employment really gainful? A student must make a certain amount in salary compared to student loan debt to be considered gainfully employed. You should not have a $50,000 loan and make a wage of $9.00 per hour after graduation. Do the math!"

The Benefit Side of the Education Equation

As the cost of education and training rises, the benefit side—namely, the increased earning potential that education theoretically provides—is arguably less solid than ever before. Wages and upward mobility for many Americans are dropping, prolonged unemployment continues to concern everybody, and recent graduates find themselves entering a tough job market. This disconnect makes being able to afford education and training all the more difficult at precisely the same time so many folks seem to need it the most.

You can see from Figure 8-1, three decades ago, recent graduate wages were on the rise at essentially the same pace as education costs. But since then, the two lines have moved in opposite directions, meaning that costs are up but earnings are down, making the considerations covered in this chapter on both the cost and benefit side of your fresh start education and training equation all the more relevant in the new economy.

It may seem as if there is little good news on the education and training front; we've only heard about rising costs, high student debt, and low wages. While getting a good return on your education investment is challenging, we can still explore some of the ways that you can "shore up" the potential benefits side of your fresh start education equation.

What the Great Recession Taught Us About Maximizing Education and Training

The good news is that America's recent unemployment challenges help to shed light on certain trends worth considering when it comes to getting a fresh start in education, training, and employment. These trends will help you make decisions that maximize the return on your education and training investment. And many of the same new economy trends that apply to your own fresh start today are equally applicable to America's next generation, perhaps your own children or grandchildren, as they plan for their own education, training, and employment tomorrow.

Following the Great Recession, millions of people found themselves without jobs, as unemployment and underemployment more than doubled from around 4 percent to more than 10 percent. More importantly, millions of folks were (and still are) without jobs for an incredibly long amount of time. Prior to the Great Recession, less than one percent of Americans were unemployed for more than twenty-four weeks (officially defined as "long-term unemployment"). In the new economy, that number has increased more than fourfold and, by some counts, is 50 percent higher if folks who've given up even looking for a job are included. What's more, many of those who've found work are working for lower wages.

Also distressing is the fact that both short- and long-term unemployment tends to be experienced disproportionately by the young, the old, the less educated, and African American and Latino workers.

Your Level of Education and Training Matters

Lesson number one from the Great Recession, and perhaps most glaring, is the difference that your level of education makes, particularly during tough employment times.

When it comes to *staying* employed during tough times, the specific level of education or training that you receive matters. The likelihood that you will remain employed when others do not increases dramatically from 93 percent with an associate degree all the way up to almost 100 percent with a doctorate degree. Folks with no high school diploma are four times as likely to be unemployed during tough times as folks with a college degree. Just graduating from high school cuts the chance of unemployment by a third.

In addition to influencing your success at staying employed, your level of education or training also impacts your income. Simply finishing high school can increase your wages by more than 38 percent, whereas completing that bachelor's degree can add as much as 41 percent over only having completed some college work and a 64 percent increase over just having a high school diploma. Perhaps more important, over the past four decades this gap has widened, a trend expected to continue in the new economy. If that's not incentive enough for folks who started but never finished an education or training program, then what is? Figure 8-2 illustrates the impact of education and training level on wages.

Figure 8-2. Your level of education in the new economy matters.

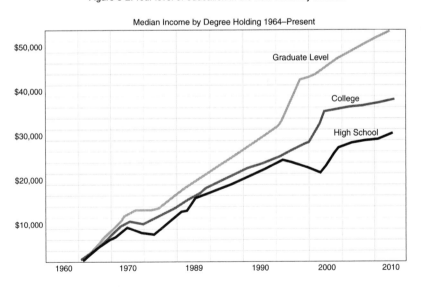

Median Income by Degree Holding 1964–Present

Your Field of Education and Training Matters

Lesson number two from the Great Recession is that your field of education and training also matters in two important ways. First, recent unemployment trends reveal that in the new economy, fields such as information technology and healthcare, for example, are among the fields that tend to be more reliable and less impacted by unemployment.

Examples of some of the fields of occupation that are expected to grow in the new economy include:

Field	Representative Jobs
Healthcare	Physical Therapist Assistants, Dental Hygienists, Veterinary Technicians, Registered Nurses, Certified Registered Nurse Anesthetists, Nurse Practitioners, Physician Assistants, Physicians, Surgeons
Financial Services	Accountants, Auditors, Actuaries, Financial Advisers
Technology	Computer Applications Specialist, Software Engineers, Systems Engineers, IT Analysts
Engineering	Project Engineers, Civil Engineers, Structural Engineers, Environmental Engineers, Biomedical Engineers
Sales	Sales Directors, Sales Executives, Retail Sales

The fields in which you may potentially seek education or training are endless, and information is available online for vocational certificates, professional licensing, and designations for most any field, from massage therapy to paralegal studies to transport. In each case, the bottom line is that your total risks and costs be considered in comparison to the benefits and return you are likely to see on that investment.

The second reason your field of education and training matters is that some jobs pay more than others. In fact, higher-earning fields can provide you with wages as much as 300 percent higher on average than lower-earning fields. Some forward-looking average incomes for top-earning fields are listed in the sidebar opposite.

Liberal arts and humanities majors tend to end up somewhere in the middle, with a median annual income of close to $50,000. Two-year degrees mirror four-year programs, with health fields leading the charts and paralegal studies following suit. The moral is that as your education, training, and employment fresh start unfolds, it is not difficult for you to access all sorts of information about the fields, levels, and types of positions predicted to be most and least in demand, pay the best wages, offer the highest reliability, and provide the most opportunity for upward mobility; you just have to know to look for it.

Beyond Level and Field: Maximizing Return on Investment in Education and Training

The combination of your level and field of education and training can have an equally stunning impact on the return on your investment. While obtaining a graduate degree, for example, does add to your earning potential, the exact extent of this effect depends on

Income by Field

Examples: Top Field by Income

Engineering: $120,000

Pharmaceutical Sciences: $105,000

Math and Computer Science: $98,000

Accounting and Finance: $60,000

Examples: Bottom Fields by Income

Counseling: $29,000

Early Childhood Education: $36,000

Theology: $38,000

Social Work: $39,000

Drama and Arts: $40,000

Studio Arts: $40,000

your field of study. Two majors that tend to consistently reach six-degree salaries immediately upon leaving graduate school in the new economy are engineering and pharmacy. Over the course of a career, the largest gain is in the general areas of healthcare and biology, with the lowest gains coming in arts and some areas of engineering. For example, folks who study the life sciences find that they can increase their average wages from $32,000 for a four-year degree to $87,000 a year by investing in a graduate degree, almost a 200 percent higher return on investment, ranking among the best return on an investment for higher education. Conversely, included among the worst return on investments in terms of wage growth by level plus field is education in the arts, where grads start out averaging $30,000 a year, growing only to around $55,000 with an advanced degree.

There are a number of other factors related to education and training that will impact your employment and income opportunities.

Performance Matters

By some estimates, students in the top 85 percent percentile of their classes can earn 10 percent to 20 percent more during their lifetime. On average that translates to a quarter of a million dollars!

Where You Get Your Education and Training Matters

Consideration of where you seek education or training is, likewise, essential. Experts warn against signing up for a program that may not deliver what it promises. For example, government reports and lawsuits have accused some for-profit institutions of doctoring attendance records or peddling near-worthless degrees. Moreover, you only get a return on your investment if you *finish* the program. Among students seeking a bachelor's degree, only 22 percent succeed within six years at for-profit institutions, compared with 65 percent at nonprofit private schools and 55 percent at public institutions. On the other hand, for-profit students tend to do better at obtaining associate degrees and certificates.

The trick with education and training is that you have to finish. When 70 percent of high school graduates enroll in some form of higher education within a year, but only 60 percent who attend four-year programs finish within six years and 20 percent in two-year programs finish within three years, the cost goes up for those that do finish, and those who do not finish are stuck with debt and no return.

Students at for-profit colleges are also twice as likely to default on their student loans. All these factors are worthy of consideration in your education and training fresh start return on investment analysis.

Paying attention to indicators—feedback from other students and graduates, dropout rates, average years to graduate, job placement records, and the like—will help you decide where to get education and training. For more information on the public vs. private school debate, check out the video clip at www.askshario.com/schooldebate.

When You Get the Training or Education Matters

If you are currently struggling with under- or unemployment, now may be an opportune time for you to reeducate or retrain since, if your earnings are down, the opportunity cost is likewise reduced. Clearly, waiting too long without a paycheck may make investing in education or training prohibitive, but in some cases you can collect unemployment and go to school at the same time.

Workers who start at lower wages tend to make less money throughout their entire earning career, and the longer you wait, the less optimal earning years you will have left. Some seniors may find themselves too far past the point of diminishing return; for them, making an investment in education or training may not be financially worth the while. On average, college graduates can expect to earn 84 percent more over their lifetime than someone with nothing more than a high school diploma. So it literally pays to invest in your education and training fresh start sooner rather than later.

No Job Is Forever

Notwithstanding the endless combination of education and training fields, levels of attainment, number of working years left, the demographics to which you belong, and even where exactly in America you live—all of which can impact your employability, wages, mobility, and job duration—the common denominators are that a prudent education, training, and employment fresh start assumes that no job is forever and that *everybody* can potentially benefit from well-planned education and training. The goal, ideally, is to position yourself so that you're always reemployable as quickly as possible, and without negatively impacting your wages.

Not Concerned About Your Own Job or Education? Why It Matters to You!

So what do education, training, and employment (or unemployment) mean to The America Company, and, as a shareholder in The America Company, why should you care? After all, even an 8 percent unemployment rate means that 92 percent of us are still gainfully employed.

For starters, you know that inflation and the cost of living is rising, particularly for essentials like food, fuel, and clothing. But did you know that since 2009, when the recovery technically began, there has been almost no increase in wages for average Americans? Carefully choosing the level and field of education that gives you the best start in wages is even more important today for everybody.

The $1 trillion balance of federal student loans is also *everybody's* problem, whether or not you are paying off loans yourself. America's student loan debt has grown by over 60 percent during the last five years alone. As many as 40 percent of all graduates delay making major purchases, such as homes and cars, because of their debt. And because folks who begin their work lives during a downturn statistically suffer adverse economic consequences for years afterward, the Great

A Matter of Life or Death

Lest anybody forget, there's far more to employment than mere money. Unemployment is almost always an emotionally traumatic event, impacting self-esteem and confidence in addition to your financial prosperity. But especially for older workers, the impacts beyond money can be serious. Experts estimate significant increases in death rates for older male workers in the years immediately following a job loss if they previously had been consistently employed. There are various reasons for this rise in mortality. One is suicide, which increases by 1.47 percent for every 10 percent increase in unemployment. Duration of unemployment is the dominant force in the relationship between joblessness and the risk of suicide. There are, likewise, links between unemployment and cancer, heart disease, and psychiatric issues. And remember, when you lose your job, you lose your healthcare coverage along with it.

The domino effect of unemployment even extends to family members, with an 18 percent increase in divorce after a husband's job loss and 13 percent after a wife's. And unemployment of parents negatively impacts their children. By some counts, kids whose fathers experience traumatic unemployment exhibit almost 10 percent lower annual earnings as adults.

Recession may still potentially be impacting twentysomethings for decades to come. You know from Chapter 1 that consumer spending accounts for 70 percent of GDP, so you know that when wages are stagnant and graduates have to repay loans rather than spend their money in The America Company's economy, this is bad news for everybody.

Washington Responds with New Rules and Reforms

Washington is aware of the benefits of education and training, and the economic impact of overwhelming student loans. Chapter 2 discussed new student loan rules and reforms. In addition, lawmakers in Washington are working to make the United States first among developed nations in college completion, and Congress has reduced the interest rates on many student loans to below commercial rates. Some of the other proposed rules and reforms related to education and training are quickly summarized for you in the next sidebar.

Help on the Front Lines

Initiatives exist at the federal, state, and local levels to assist with training and retraining, but needs exceed resources and they can change at any time, so again time is not on your side and, if you are suffering, the time to seek this retraining fresh start assistance is now.

Laid-off workers, often with family responsibilities that interfere with class schedules, are more likely to require financial aid and are more prone to need help with basic reading, writing, and math, creating challenges that aren't encountered as much with younger workers. Some aid is provided at the state level with backing from the U.S. Department of Labor Office of Workforce Investment (OWI). OWI provides leadership, oversight, policy guidance, and assistance under the Workforce Investment Act of 1998—for example, Trade Adjustment Assistance programs. The Trade Adjustment Assistance Extension Act of 2011 changed eligibility requirements, benefits, and service created to help workers unemployed because of the effects of international trade. "Rapid Response," for example, was designed to assist with plant closings and layoffs by providing resources through One-Stop Career Centers that include résumé and interview

Examples of Proposed Education and Training Rules and Reforms

- Increase federal aid to colleges and universities that keep tuition affordable, provide good value, and serve needy students, and reduce federal aid to those that do not.

- Create special incentives for states and colleges to keep costs under control. Utilize Supplemental Educational Opportunity Grants (SAGO), Perkins loans, and revised formulas for distributing work study and expansion of loans in the federal Perkins program.

- Support public and private colleges and nonprofit organizations that are developing and testing strategies to boost higher education attainment and student outcomes and productivity. Strategies include redesigning courses to enhance teaching and learning; making better use of education technology; providing early college preparation activities to lessen the need for remediation; supporting competency-based approaches to gaining college credit; and other ideas aimed at spurring changes in the culture of higher education.

- Use a College Scorecard that provides essential information about college costs, graduation rates, and potential earnings. The scorecard is an easy-to-read format and updated version of a required "Financial Aid Shopping Sheet." The idea is to make it easier for families to compare college financial aid packages and begin collecting earnings and employment information for colleges, so that students can have an even better sense of the postgraduation outcomes they can expect.

- Increase Pell grants, shore up the direct loan and income-based repayment programs, keep interest rates low (including interest rates on subsidized Stafford student loans to avoid doubling from 3.4 percent to 6.8 percent), make the American Opportunity Tax Credit permanent, and double the number of work-study jobs over the next five years.

workshops, new skills training and job counseling, and community college and career training grant programs. The Adult and Dislocated Worker program (under Title I of the Workforce Investment Act) was likewise designed to provide for employment and training to assist you in finding employment, if you qualify, and helps employers find skilled workers. Each state crafts its own specific programs and is responsible for management and operations. Employer Worker Training grants and on-the-job training were designed to provide funding for companies to pay for training to advance current employees and retrain for jobs. Incumbent Worker Training programs were designed to pay for customized training to teach existing employees new skills for promotion and to increase productivity and retention. And Quick Response Training programs were designed to provide custom training for new or expanding businesses in order to allow some states to attract and retain high-quality jobs. By some counts, dislocated workers who retrain are 4 percent more likely to find a job than those who do not, and earn $1,200 more per year.

The Bottom Line: Paying It Forward

It appears that The America Company underestimated the impact that technology, globalization, and other changes over the past years were going to have on average folks' wages, employment, and, ultimately, upward mobility. In what now seems like the blink of an eye, average American workers were thrust into the workforce boxing ring with billions of global human worker competitors and endless computerized and mechanized competitors. As workers' wages in other countries have grown, increasing an average of eightfold, American workers' wages in the new economy continue to stumble. The result, as shown in Figure 8-3, is that in the new economy the United States has less

Why Reeducation and Retraining Are Needed Now More Than Ever

The first public employment programs in the United States were created in response to the Great Depression. Although successful, these efforts, notably the Civilian Conservation Corps and the Works Progress Administration, were largely terminated when the country entered World War II and the Depression ended. The federal government did not become involved in education and training programs like that again until 1961, revisiting the subject at least a half dozen times since, but still not with the outcomes The America Company needs and is capable of achieving.

The creation of America's middle class didn't just happen. It was the result of deliberate initiatives crafted to sustainably improve lives, to help folks help themselves and their families. Unlike the olden days when education was for the rich, after the war, America's middle class was provided with public educational and training institutions and enjoyed rising wages and upward mobility. Unlike some other forms of public assistance, education is the help that keeps on giving since children of educated folks are more likely to become educated as well, and so on. Fast-forward to the new economy where, in large part due to debt and budget constraints covered in Chapter 1, The America Company now spends almost $1 billion less on retraining the unemployed than it did a decade ago when the unemployment rate was less than half of what it is today.

opportunity for upward mobility than France, Germany, Sweden, Canada, Finland, Norway, and Denmark.

Figure 8-3. The U.S. has less relative mobility than many of the other industrialized nations.

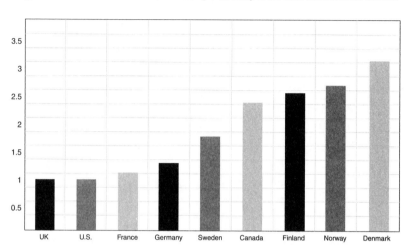

For Americans, these figures are troubling not just because we are losing ground, but because of what it means to our children. The generations before us believed, and rightly so, that their children would have more opportunities than they had enjoyed; each generation knew that the next generation would move up, be wealthier, and enjoy a great panoply of careers from which to choose. The America Company is responding with the initiatives discussed in this chapter. But it is up to each of us, the stakeholders in The America Company, to take matters in hand and invest wisely in our own individual education and training, striving to go to the right schools and choose fields of opportunity. After all, it is with education that sustainable prosperity is launched. A generation ago, the percentage of graduates in America ranked among the highest in the world. But while other nations and their shareholders went the extra mile, collectively improving education rates by 15 percent, the education levels of Americans flatlined. As a result, America now ranks number nine in percentage of graduates. And it's happened while the very best educational institutions in the world can be found smack-dab in America's own backyard!

America was the land where professional opportunities and the chance for upward mobility were available to all. The founding members of our American communities came to this far-off, unknown land seeking only one thing: a chance at a fresh start. Today, Chinese students, for example, come to America to study, and then return to their own country because there are more professional opportunities there than America can now offer.

Surviving the Great Recession and thriving in the new economy requires the resilience for which Americans are known. That's what a fresh start is all about. The potentially life-changing impact that millions of education, training, and employment fresh starts can have over time is undeniable. The America Company and its shareholders will bounce back from the challenges of today's democracy the way they always have: one fresh start at a time.

Conclusion

As you've progressed through the five steps of your financial fresh start, you've connected the dots between what happens in Washington, on Wall Street, and inside homes across America with your own financial prosperity. You now know why respectable wages for The America Company's workers—wages that at least keep pace with inflation—are essential to The America Company's economy and your own financial well-being. Businesses cannot afford to produce products and services if folks can't afford to buy them, and encouraging folks to borrow in order to do that and make ends meet just didn't work. This situation may, over time, require everybody to step up, "buy American," and perhaps pay a little more at the cash register. After all, it's going to cost us all one way or another, and you know that what's good for The America Company is generally good for your own wallet, and vice versa.

Respectable jobs and wages, which go hand in hand with opportunity for upward mobility, are the most fundamental element of average Americans' hopes and dreams. A *country,* by definition, cannot have its own hopes and dreams. A country's hopes and dreams come from its *people,* and the more people who believe in and share those hopes and dreams, the more real they become. In fact, it has been said that these aspirations, not actual, measurable, current conditions like GDP or wages, define a nation and its future. That's how important average Americans' collective hopes and dreams are. Yet as you have seen, hopes and dreams are becoming increasingly elusive for folks in the new economy.

At the end of the day, The America Company is *you,* times the other 300-million-plus people who together comprise Americans and who together once made America great and who together can do it again. The financial challenges for average Americans and The America Company, including global competition, are not mutually exclusive. It can no longer be taken for granted that America will remain the leader among nations indefinitely or, as the value of the U.S. dollar continues to decline (see Figure C-1), that the U.S. dollar will continue being accepted as the universal global currency forever.

Figure C-1. Value of U.S. dollar.

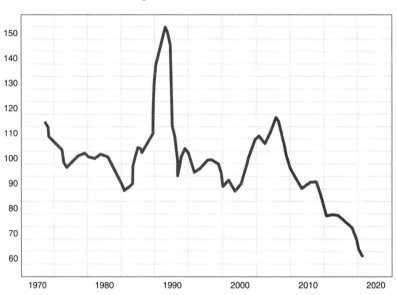

The value of the U.S. dollar has declined.

In the quest to overcome these challenges, you are The America Company's most valuable resource. Of course, succeeding in your five-step fresh start plan helps you, but it helps America, too. The country, plainly, can't do it without you. That's good news for all of us if you are prepared to rise to the occasion and bad news if you are not.

This is not the first time Americans have been challenged, and it certainly won't be the last. In fact, I imagine you will agree that today's challenges pale in comparison to those faced by the Founding Fathers the Civil War generation or even my grandfather. As you embark on your own financial fresh start, perhaps you will keep in mind the many other opportunities it also presents for you to "do the right thing" in terms of your personal expectations and responsibilities, not the least of which are the financial values, attitudes, and impressions you choose to teach your own children, your legacy, and The America Company's next generation of shareholders. For more information on the legacy you leave your children, see the video clip at www. askshario.com/teachingkids.

A Very Simple Answer

This book began by asking a very simple question. How commonplace will the occurrences we are witnessing today—foreclosure, people strategically deciding not to pay back debts, cities and towns going bankrupt, huge financial institutions and even entire countries being bailed out—be ten years from now? Will the America we pass on still be the greatest nation in the world? The very simple answer is that it all depends on you.

Index